YOUR OWN PONY CLUB

# YOUR OWN PONY CLUB

A practical guide to keeping ponies on a shoe-string budget

*by*

JUDITH CAMPBELL

LUTTERWORTH PRESS

GUILDFORD AND LONDON

*First published* 1979



ISBN 0 7188 2371 0



PRINTED PHOTOLITHO IN GREAT BRITAIN
BY EBENEZER BAYLIS AND SON LTD
THE TRINITY PRESS, WORCESTER, AND LONDON

## CONTENTS

CONTENTS

## ACKNOWLEDGEMENTS

The author wishes to thank most sincerely those parents, friends, pony-owners and riders who helped to make the Twala Club such a success. The publishers and author also wish to acknowledge the following for permission for the use of their photographs: Sheila Adams (p. 96); *Folkestone Herald and Gazette* (p. 125); Sue Godden (pp. 46, 51, 53 and 78); W. S. Pearson (p. 139); George Rodger (pp. 15, 25, 32, 37, 41, 65, 89, 96, 115, 119, 121, and 123); Tony Stanton (pp. 8, 58, 68, 75 and 134); Robert Tait (pp. 48, 101 and 136); Peter F. Wiggins (p. 13).

1. *The President. Twala, our family pony for 25 years, enjoys attending club shows.*

# FOREWORD

"Ponyitis" is a common disease and one, at any rate in our family, that appears to be incurable. In theory my pony era came to an end when our daughters left home and their ponies went to new owners. But Twala, that four-footed member of the family for some twenty-eight years, remained as my own mount and, although long retired, is still with us. And today, more by accident than design, there are six other ponies as well.

Few of the many odd things that have happened to me down the years have been due to any premeditated plan of action, and this influx of equines is no exception. It is true they are the core of a shoe-string riding club for local children, a club to which Twala, as president, has given his name. But the club came about as the chance result of my noticing that after school the young people of this hamlet tended to stand around in aimless groups, with apparently nothing much to do and nowhere much to go. And since it seems to me that the young of today are deprived of much of the legitimate adventure and challenge open to previous generations, on impluse I asked a few if they would be interested in learning to ride.

The response, if not over-enthusiastic, was mostly acquiescent and the idea culminated in my toting eight young people, surprisingly with boys in the majority, to a local riding school for a lesson one evening a week.

During the ensuing months we had our ups and downs—a number of literal "downs"—and a good deal of morale-boosting on my part was necessary to keep the interest going. One participant did opt out before the course was finished; a couple vanished as soon as it was, but in the mean time there were others to replace them and the general opinion seemed to be that riding was worth while and quite good fun.

By the time the riding school phase came to an end there was a nucleus of ten young people, two thirds of them boys, who had acquired the first rudiments of the sport. And that was the moment when it became apparent that the matter could not be allowed to rest there. This little group might have discovered an enjoyable pastime, but none were in a position to follow it up through owning a pony of their own, or even continuing with instruction unless it was still sponsored. And if they were then abandoned in mid-air, so to speak, their original boredom would be coupled with frustration and their plight worse than before.

Something had to be done. So, with the aid of Twala, brought out of semi-retirement for a while, and the then recently acquired Aunt Jabiska, the Twala Club staggered into being—with little idea of how it would function, what it might achieve, or how long it could survive.

Now, more than six years later and still to my surprise, the club continues to flourish. There is a permanent waiting list, and on the credit side are the thirty-four or so young people who through the years have acquired something of horsemanship and horse-sense and, I hope, an undying taste for all the fun and good qualities that go along with horses and ponies.

And, thinking about it all, it occurs to me that there must be numerous people, perhaps retired or semi-retired, with far more knowledge and time than I have, who might like to try their hand at something similar. I have therefore attempted to set down some of the basic requirements, the pitfalls and the many rewards attached to running a shoe-string little experiment in communal pony keeping.

Obviously different circumstances would make for many variations on the same theme, although in the interests of the ponies it would I think be impossible to be more financially "rock-bottom" than the Twala Club. If the idea could not be down-graded, however, with better facilities and a larger cash flow it would be easy to improve upon.

And from a purely personal angle I would like to assure any would-be promoters of such a scheme, that while the Twala Club does demand a lot of time, hard work, and occasional anxiety, it also remains an endless source of interest, amusement and fun.

# *Chapter One*

## BEGINNINGS

### *AIMS*

UNFORTUNATELY INFLATION HAS not bypassed any aspect of the horse world. Nowadays the initial cost of a very ordinary type of pony is sufficient to put off many deserving families who would provide good homes. But even where a pony is forthcoming and there are adequate facilities, it is the day-to-day running costs that so often make the whole idea impossible.

Keeping ponies collectively, at a ratio of so many riders per pony, is obviously much cheaper than going it alone. An association like the Twala Club can therefore help solve the purely financial problem, but there is a great deal more to such a club than that.

Despite the monetary angle, and the paradoxical circumstance of our living in a nuclear age, it is said there are more horses and ponies in the British Isles now than for the past fifty years. This is mostly due to the increasing interest in riding and connected sports amongst people of all age groups and walks of life, but those who can afford to keep a horse or pony are not always those who merit them. Unhappily enthusiasm alone does not ensure understanding and correct care. And if there are too many instances where the knowledgeable cannot afford the pony they deserve, equally there are too many homes where the animal may be genuinely "loved", but where through ignorance it receives treatment that amounts to neglect, sometimes to unintentional cruelty.

Whatever else the Twala Club may be, it is not a method of obtaining riding "on the cheap" through the exploitation of the ponies involved. Under supervision the members are responsible for the care and well-being of the animals, all of which are on loan. And while the club rides with enjoyment and competes with zest, pony-care and all that that entails figures equally, if not more, prominently. Nor does this side of it stop at the actual health and well-being of the ponies—with finances as "shoe-string" as ours, everything from building shelters and erecting fences to making hay has to be undertaken by the members and their families.

A weekly lesson from a qualified instructor has been one of the highlights for the past two years, but otherwise the members have to ride unattended, and the older and more experienced are expected to help the novices. All these various facets of the club help members to become both reliable and self-reliant—while an unexpected bonus is that because parents are so good at "mucking in" with the chores and general running of the club, it has become very much a family affair.

## *FINDING OUR FEET*

Before the club existed as such, Twala and his lately acquired field-mate, Jabiska, were used to supplement our professional riding school instruction with a little practical horse-sense. None of our riders comes from a horse background, and this "homework" was, for instance, of great assistance in the beginning when the school expected all pupils, after brief instruction, to tack up their own animals before a class. In the early days, unless someone could get around to give all of them a hand, this led to some odd situations. Ponies appeared with apparently only one ear, the other crumpled up under the head-piece of the bridle, throat-lashes were commonly tightened to suffocation point, and on one memorable occasion one of our boys led his mount into the school with its saddle on back to front. It was therefore very helpful to be able to practise the mysteries of saddling and bridling quietly at home. And here Twala, who has never suffered the painful indignity of having his teeth bashed with the bit, was always co-operative about opening his mouth even for the most microscopic rider—although he might nip a protest if girthed too vigorously.

2. *Running a club also means lending a hand! Jason being trimmed.*

Jabiska made no bones about being saddled, however clumsily, but merely clenched her ancient teeth if the bridling was not performed to her liking.

These short periods of trial and error at home were also utilized to solve problems like that of one of our girls, in theory the keenest rider of the bunch, who in practice turned out to be so paralytically nervous that she was holding up the class by a total inability to learn to rise at the trot. This dilemma was resolved by putting her and Jabiska on a lead and someone jogging on foot beside them round the lanes, intoning "Up . . . down! Up . . . down!" It was breathless work and for a time our rider still shrieked and clutched the unprotesting mare by the ears if she so much as sneezed, but success came eventually. And not so many years later it was rewarding when that particular rider was able to take up, and enjoy, the offer of hunting quite a "hot" pony.

In sessions such as these we came to appreciate that different methods work with different characters. At a later date the same trouble, on this occasion with a boy, was dealt with by bawling in sergeant-major tones: "If you're not rising properly when you've circled the field, you're out of the Twala Club!" That worked well, too.

## *STARTING UP*

By the time the school instruction came to an end and the club was at least in embryonic form, I had a faint idea of what can be expected of inexperienced riders newly out on their own and lacking the safe confines of an indoor school. It also soon became evident that on this score any suppositions need to be kept permanently elastic—as even after a while in the club it is remarkable what members can get up to.

There was the day when a much loved but sadly outgrown pony was to go off to a new home chosen by his owner. It was inevitable that when his new family arrived to see and collect him Spot should have mysteriously put on a couple of hundredweight during the night. But this alone did not seem sufficient reason for his reluctance to approach, let alone jump, an eighteen-inch pole when the previous week he had blithely jumped clear round a novice course, as is his wont. Fortunately his would-be owners accepted my embarrassed assurances that this was not his normal form, and the mystery was solved when we unbridled him. The enthusiastic Twala Clubber who had tacked him up, had previously, quite rightly, taken the bridle to pieces to ensure its cleanliness for such an important occasion . . . but had put the bit back upside down!

There was another memorable day when Paint, brought in from a ride by someone who did not normally go out alone, was accused of "being naughty and running away!" In his youth Paint was known to take hold a little when hunting, but this description of his behaviour in no way fitted our elderly, dependable piebald. And I must confess that words did not fail me when on further questioning it transpired that the pony had been expected to wait, untied and unattended, in an unfenced car-park while his rider ascertained the opening time of the local wild-life sanctuary.

But then, horse-sense is inborn only to the fortunate few. And why should the majority of the young of today, geared to machines from birth, be expected to have the horse-sense so instinctive to their forbears? Instilling horse-sense, an understanding of what a pony is likely to do next, and what to do about it if it does, is one of the most important functions of the club. To some the understanding comes quickly; others are slow to the point of despair, but patience does have its reward. And that is the moment when, apparently overnight, an irresponsible, scatter-brained eleven-year-old, hitherto scarcely to be trusted out of sight, shows unmistakable signs of becoming a dependable, knowledgeable horseman (or should it be horse-person?)

3. *This trio of boys soon outgrew Spotty and Paint.*

By and large, it says a great deal for the young people who have in turn embarked on this experiment, and certainly as much for the various ponies who co-operate so happily, that to date there have been no serious disasters. With few exceptions all of it has been successful to some degree, and usually enjoyable.

*BASICS*

Even with a venture as shoe-string as ours, it would be impossible to get off the ground without a few essential facilities, and without first making some basic decisions.

Whatever the number of ponies at any one time, there must be at least minimal grazing, with water available and adequate fencing.

Each pony has to be furnished with tack which, if not of the most modern pattern, must be correctly fitting and safe. And there has to be somewhere conveniently placed and secure in which to keep the tack.

When it comes to the ponies, whether like ours they are on loan or whether they belong to the club, they have to be of the right size and temperament for those who will ride them—and this is particularly important during the first year or so when everyone is finding his way, and chances cannot be taken.

As for rules, even if, as we found, these need to be altered and adapted later according to circumstances, there must be a core of regulations, clearly understood if not actually written down, that will as far as possible ensure the safety and well-being of riders and ponies alike.

Last, but unfortunately not least, ways and means of financing the club sufficiently to cover expenses have to be thought up and acted upon.

As for myself, since this adventure was as new to me as to those for whose benefit it was intended, like them I have had to find my way. As I was responsible from the start for a number of other people's children, and ponies, it was immediately necessary to establish an overall authority—while trying to avoid the easy trap of becoming too "bossy". And whatever the circumstances, it falls to the lot of whoever runs such a club to generate enthusiasm when necessary, iron out the difficulties, and generally keep it all moving along.

In some ways the early days were easier than now. Although the liability was greater, my task then consisted principally of saying: "Do this, do that . . .", or, far more frequently: "DON'T do" one or the other!

Now, with a nucleus of increasingly experienced and reliable members, it is often a question of trying to judge when and how far to loosen the rein and delegate more of the responsibility. There have been mistakes on both sides, but future planning and decision-making are gradually being taken over by those who are most concerned. Recently four "leaders" have been appointed, chosen for age and/or experience. They take it in turns to organize gangs of the other members for coping with the weekly chores previously initiated by myself, and are now responsible for seeing that all the dull essentials, fence checking and mending, paddock weeding, dung collecting etc., are dealt with as a matter of course. This takes a lot off my shoulders, and it is a joy to be able to hand over confidently on such occasions as organizing the club to compete at a gymkhana—a job that requires tact as well as horse-sense, and is no simple task when riders of varying ability but equal keenness outnumber ponies by at least two to one!

During the past seven years we have all learned a great deal, not least the realization that the fun of being involved with ponies is inexhaustible. And even the newest member can appreciate the joke of the boy who, after six months with us, announced he was leaving because: "Now I can ride, I think I'll learn to skate!"

## *Chapter Two*

# FACILITIES

### *GRAZING*

FIRST THINGS FIRST, and if the couple of small fields already available were adequate for the two ponies with which we started, we realized directly it was certain that the club was established that there would soon have to be more animals —and we had to have somewhere to keep them.

Limited time and, during the school terms, limited help, mean that, whatever the dreams of keeping stabled ponies, there is only one method for the club animals, and that is keeping them out at grass all year round. And for this to be practicable, both for the members and myself, it is essential that they are kept within half a mile of my home. It is unfortunate that our farm should be twelve miles from where we live so that, although Twala is living out his days there, for club purposes that grazing is inaccessible. And in this locality, as in so many, it is a permanent problem.

So, until our recent acquisition of larger acreage, the six Twala Club ponies were juggled around a miscellany of small loaned or rented plots and fields, all within the prescribed radius, totalling no more than seven and a half acres of mostly not very good pasture.

By any standards that is scarcely luxurious acreage for that number of animals, but although the period between January and the coming of the spring grass annually produced a near crisis, somehow it was contrived so that no pony suffered in any way from lack of grazing. The larger acreage that we have now acquired cuts down the winter work, as well as some of the expense of the extra hay and concentrates necessary when there is nothing for the ponies to forage, but we did prove that with care and good management it is possible for ponies to thrive on about one acre per head, an area that on paper appears inadequate.

Trying to find additional grazing was always a club top priority, and the extra three and a half acres is making life considerably easier. Our fields, however, still bear no relation to the big, rolling pastures of our dreams, and through the years we have learned that the key to keeping ponies well and healthy on small plots is strict field maintenance.

### *ROTATION*

Usually the ponies are divided into the groups that best agree, the size of the group determined by the size of the field, and switched from field to field in order to rest each parcel of grazing in turn. The normal poaching of the ground in winter is obviously a worse problem on small areas, and not helped by the fact that the wetter the ground the more our ponies appear to delight in playing and galloping about.

### *WEED CONTROL*

If funds and space allowed, each field would be ploughed and re-seeded in turn with a suitable grass-cum-herbage mixture to ensure maximum good grazing. It would then be possible to take a hay crop from more than one field, which would in turn assist in controlling red-worm, and is a project to be attempted at the first financial opportunity. As it is we do our best to improve what we have, and annual weed spraying and pulling is one of the most important routine jobs.

Not many years ago our largest field (two and a quarter acres), like the smallest (a flat three-quarters of an acre used mostly for schooling and jumping), was arable land growing strawberries commercially. A small portion of the larger one reverted to pasture through the natural seeding of wild grasses, unfortunately of little nutritional value, and the remainder was ploughed and re-sown. Through a misunderstanding the grass mixture was more suited to sheep than horses, and in spring the large proportion of clover scoured the ponies and increased the risk of laminitis. As this field has to produce part of our annual hay crop, an additional problem was that the clover hay, although much relished and with a beautiful "nose" to it, was very dusty. And for no apparent reason the field also grew an abundant selection of docks.

An annual application of a systemic weed-killer, applied by slogging up and down the steep gradient with a knapsack sprayer, eventually eliminated the docks and, assisted by the fierce heat of the summer of '76, reduced the clover to required proportions. A welcome gift of grass-seed, sown by hand, filled in the gaps left by the defunct docks and supplemented the feeding value of the wild grasses. This field now produces good grazing for much of the year and, weather permitting, three or more tons of quite good hay.

The smaller fields, where weeds seem to flourish, are also sprayed at intervals and "hand pulled". Mixed herbage containing some of the "safe" vetches, a proportion of dandelions and other similar delicacies, makes good grazing for native-bred ponies, and in moderation nettles that have been cut and left to dry are appreciated. But thistles and docks and burdock, plants such as the grass-smothering chick-weed, and of course any weeds poisonous to ponies, have to be summarily dealt with. Ragwort can be a recurring bugbear but does respond to being pulled by hand. Now it is a matter of routine, but the worst field was cleared originally by organizing a ragwort party—with a small prize for the largest bundles, suitable refreshments for the workers and two or three reliable leaders to ensure that all the plants were removed from the field so that they would not dry and tempt the ponies to eat them.

Some of the fields grow clumps of coarse grass that the ponies will not touch and where they commonly dung, which increases the problem. Raking between these tufts and then cutting them with shears is an effective but back-breaking remedy, and a better one is to find an old-timer expert with a scythe. If these areas are cut regularly for a time the ponies will normally start to graze them, and since, unlike lawn-mowings which quickly heat, the cut grass is safe for them to eat, it can be left in the field.

*FERTILIZING*

Within reason, and bearing in mind that ponies are not cattle, the more nitrogen applied to a field the better the crop of grass, but we are limited to what we can afford or come by. The bulk of our fertilizer has to be put on the would-be hay field, and any left over is eked out amongst the remaining acres. Kind farmers sometimes give us a sack or two to supplement what the club can buy. And rubbish-dumps can be a fruitful source of bags of the stuff that has become lumpy and been discarded but can be reduced to a usable state again with energetic pounding by club members.

Occasionally we are able to borrow sufficient grazing for the ponies for a couple of weeks during the crucial time at the end of March/beginning of April. This means that there is then a heaven-sent opportunity to tidy up our own fields, fertilize and "patch seed" them, and even this short respite from grazing makes all the difference to the eventual crop of grass.

*DUNG*

Manure is an inevitable and ceaseless by-product of keeping ponies and, whatever the size of the fields, one that has to be dealt with. On large acreages it can be scattered by raking or harrowing, but if small areas are not to become impossibly worm-ridden, horse-sick and eventually useless, the dung has got to be collected up regularly and removed.

It is no good pretending that anyone enjoys this job, and Twala Clubbers are no exception. However, their lack of enthusiasm, especially noticeable on cold, dank days in winter, has now been stemmed to a degree by exploiting a ready market for the product amongst local gardeners.

The dung is collected into plastic sacks, the type originally filled with fertilizer or seed, of which farmers are only too glad to be relieved, and as these are waterproof they can be stored in the open during the slacker selling periods. Sold at 25p per bag this makes a surprisingly worthwhile addition to club funds. And by setting aside 25p out of every £1's worth each member collects, to put against future entry fees at gymkhanas, an incentive has been created that works quite well.

If our fields were larger, the rougher grazing would benefit materially from introducing a few cattle for the occasional week to eat off the coarse grasses the ponies ignore, and ingest, in their case harmlessly, the eggs and larvae of red-worm—but space really precludes the experiment.

## *FENCING*

Fencing, and repairing it, is a chore that never seems to come to an end. And it took our originally unhorse-minded parents, who have to cope with it, a long while to appreciate just how strong and Houdini-like ponies are.

Some years ago Twala, who suffers from mild sweet-itch, caused consternation in the village by rubbing his backside against an electricity supply pole erected in his field. It was a very solid affair, but "gave" sufficiently to Twala's satisfying exertions to set all the cables swinging to and fro, emitting a display of sparks reminiscent of bonfire night. These high jinks have nothing to do with an actual fence, but the story demonstrates the strength generated by even half a ton of cob!

Spotty was one of those characters who remain in a field only as long as they wish to. One day when he was obviously bored, he was seen to back himself up the field, put his head down and charge the tall but rather ancient wattle that served as a gate. Two attacks were sufficient to break the lower rungs. He then completed the job by getting down on his knees, inserting head and neck under the remains, and pushing until the wreckage was resting flat on his back so that he could wriggle out to pursue his quest for pastures new. A strip of wire-netting across the replacement wattle, kept in place by a couple of strands of barbed wire, put paid to that particular exit, but Spotty usually came up with a new scheme before very long.

It has long been a private dream of mine that I will one day own acres and acres of perfect horse pasture, all enclosed by wooden posts and rails. But dreams are no better at materializing for me than for most people, and in the mean time for fencing we make do mainly with that bane of all good horsemen, barbed wire.

### *BARBED WIRE*

If the ponies were blood animals, or scatty by nature, or very young, this type of fencing could not be contemplated. But so long as it is taut and the lower strand no less than eighteen inches from the ground, "family" ponies like ours do appear to appreciate its dangers and live with it in safety. As a form of fencing it is no longer cheap, but it is at least less expensive than other kinds. It is also easy to erect. Where barbed wire is unforgiveably dangerous is where it is slack, or loose, as the scars above Jason's off-fore heel demonstrate, or has been used to supplement a gappy hedge that has then in part grown up around it.

There was an unforgettable day when I saw Jabiska standing unnaturally still, head on to the hedgerow. She whinnied, and as I approached I saw that Spotty, her companion, was in the next meadow. He had managed to jump there without much effort, but the mare's courage had apparently failed as she tried to follow, and she was inextricably held by strands of barbed wire, invisible amongst the brambles, that were looped round her forelegs.

There was nothing with which to hold her and she started to struggle when I moved away, so I was forced to squat more or less underneath her chest and try to "talk her down". Slowly and gently one leg was disentangled, and she was then persuaded to hold it up out of harm's way until the other was freed. It must have taken ten long minutes to achieve, and if she had struggled her legs would have been lacerated. But she had been sufficiently intelligent and trusting to do exactly what was required, and if the proceedings confirmed my dislike of barbed wire, the memory of that old mare's sense and co-operation keeps her a special place in my affections long after she is gone.

As many owners have discovered to their cost, barbed wire fences play havoc with New Zealand rugs because ponies that wear them soon learn that they can then lean on the stuff with impunity. The big Welsh cob, Jason, grows a fine, silky coat that in winter necessitates his wearing one of these rugs. The damage he contrives to do to the tough canvas is exasperating and he has more or less shredded a couple that were not in their first youth, but his discovery of the ease with which he can lean on barbed wire to graze the other side of the fence has more sinister aspects.

It was late one Christmas Eve when we heard the thunderous sound of a horse going flat out down the steep hill on which we live. There is only one local animal capable of producing quite such a clatter, and, dashing out, we were just in time to see, illumined in the headlights of a following car, the unmistakable outline of Jason's back end, rug flapping in the slip-stream as he rounded the corner at the foot of the hill on his way to join some friends.

On investigation we discovered that someone had inadvertently removed a post that was acting as kingpin to our fencing, and Jason had been leaning harder and harder on the wire in order to graze a neighbour's lawn until the angle suggested it was jumpable. Happily no harm came to the cob from his midnight sortie, but we refrained from inquiring into the state of the lawn after his soup-plate feet had carried him up it at the gallop.

### *SHELTER*

If ponies are to live out through the winter, there must be shelter of some kind from wind and driving rain even if they only stand up against it. Apart from other considerations, it is poor economy if the animal has to expend much of the energy

4. *Ponies living out need shelter. This useful complex was built by the club families.*

derived from its food on trying to keep warm—and cold horses, like cold humans, do not thrive. Despite all the cosseting she received, and the use of a hunter-'chaser's stable if she wished, Aunt Jabiska, who grew a surfeit of unwanted hair on her legs but little enough elsewhere, in winter looked a disgrace to the club until also provided with a warm New Zealand rug.

Native-bred ponies—the hardy little Exmoors and Dartmoors, the New Foresters, Welsh and the rest of them—can usually make do with a thick hedge or side of a house as a windbreak. But, even if it is only used regularly in summer to get away from the flies, on a dirty cold night the knowledge that an open shed is available if required is as comforting to the owner as to the pony.

Our shelters range from the smart stable that Jabiska utilized, to a curious edifice that was a chicken-house when I was a small girl—and that is a long time ago. The doorway to this lodging has sunk with the years, but even the largest of our animals is adept at lowering himself sufficiently to get inside when he wants to. One small field, apart from being south-facing and flanked by a wood, has no other shelter to date, but is not used when wind and weather are unsuitable.

Our most satisfactory protection is that included in an ambitious complex recently designed and erected by club fathers from timber and galvanized-iron sheeting salvaged from demolition sites. It consists of two open shelters, one sufficiently large for two or three ponies to squabble in in safety, and an adjacent smaller one, with access through it to the hay store that runs all along the back of the buildings. The tack-room is enclosed within the complex, with a door opening into the larger shed so that ponies can be tied up, groomed and saddled in comfort—a marvellous luxury for anyone who has ever had to saddle up in the open, regardless of weather.

## *TACK-ROOM*

The gift of a few sheets of Perspex made it possible to let panels into the roof of both hay store and tack-room so that they are well lighted. And the acquisition of a well-appointed dry place in which to keep the tack under proper conditions, does also have a psychologically good effect on those who are supposed to clean it!

Each pony's saddle and bridle (most of them lent with the animal and of good design and make), have their own home-made rack and hook, with name attached. There is an ancient wooden "horse" for cleaning saddles, and a composite hook for the bridles—both relics of my childhood. An ex-wardrobe, minus door but with shelves for saddle soap, grooming kit, bandages, first-aid and this and that, and space for hanging surplus tack, makes it easier to keep the place tidy. A large open chest is used for storing what rugs we possess, and a long working bench with space above for notices, plus the refinement of a mirror, completes the fittings.

Unlike the shelters, which stand on earth and are bedded with an unlimited supply of straw from the farm, the tack-room has a wooden floor that greatly helps in keeping it moderately warm and dry.

Security, a matter of great importance nowadays, is taken care of by a padlocked door and an efficient burglar-alarm.

## *WATER*

This is one of the most essential facilities, and it would be pleasant if each field were supplied by a clear-running stream with a firm approach to the drinking spot. As they are not we have to think again, but the members of the Twala Club are luckier than my daughters were when they were young. In those days there was an enormous field in which to keep their four ponies—but every drop of water had to be humped by bucket.

Now good neighbours undertake to supply water to the fields adjoining them—and that despite the fact that, like Twala before them, most of the ponies are not above banging on an empty container, regardless of the hour, should their needs have for once been overlooked. A stand-pipe and hose supply the largest and smallest of the fields as they are on opposite sides of the same lane. Another large cistern is filled up each weekend by means of a "Heath Robinson" collection of hose-pipes bridging the long gap twixt tap and container.

Our basic facilities have been acquired, built up or improved through the years as the number of ponies and our requirements increased. None of it is luxurious and most of it makeshift, but it is adequate and the ponies' condition and behaviour bears this out.

## *Chapter Three*

# ACQUIRING PONIES

A CLUB SIMILAR to the Twala Club but better endowed financially might be able to buy its own animals, but in our case there has never been any question of doing it that way. With the exception of Twala, Jabiska, and the other two belonging to me, all the club ponies have been loaned from outside sources—and this has been the great slice of good luck that has enabled the club to continue and expand.

### *INDEFINITE LOAN*

For various reasons, often loss of keep, the rising costs of feeding a pony or the fact that it is outgrown, many people are faced with the problem of being unable to retain the favourite that they cannot bear to sell. A number of owners resort to solving the problem by placing their ponies on "indefinite loan". Often this solution works admirably, but it can be a fiasco if a few commonsensical safeguards are not observed by both sides to the bargain.

### *LENDERS*

There are nasty stories of ponies, shunted off to a borrower without adequate previous inquiries, landing up in downright bad or unsuitable homes. Unscrupulous people have been known to take an animal on loan and then re-"lend" it anywhere they can—at a profit. Some unfortunate horses and ponies have been sold, or even put down, without their owners' knowledge. In extreme cases, apparently genuine "borrowers", only too happy to show off a home with good facilities to the pony's owner, within hours of the animal's arrival have sent it on its way to the profitable Continental horseflesh market.

## *BORROWERS*

On the other hand, the bad transactions are not entirely one-sided. Those on the receiving end have occasionally found themselves lumbered with an unsound animal described as fit for their requirements, or one with some unmentioned vice that makes it quite unsuitable for the purpose for which it is wanted, only to discover that its owner, conscience presumably salved by not having actually sold it, has either disappeared or is exceptionally loath to take it back.

Life being what it is, owners wishing to lend a pony should realize that the perfect home is not easy to find, and from the borrower's angle loaned horses and ponies can scarcely be expected to measure up exactly to the recipient's dream. But with good will and commonsense investigation on both sides, plus a few rational provisos, an indefinite loan should be a very happy arrangement. Almost without exception we have found it so.

## *WAYS AND MEANS*

Apart from my own, two of our borrowed ponies were local products. Briggy, whose stay was sadly curtailed by advancing age, came from friends. Amber, like Briggy an "outgrown", was the result of Twala Club requirements being circulated on the local grapevine; and Jason, although hailing from further afield, was acquired in much the same way. His owner had had him since a foal and, no longer able to ride, could not contemplate selling him. She knew of the Twala Club and had heard from the friend of a friend that we were in need of something approximating to Jason's generous dimensions.

Acquiring a pony in this way presents few problems because there is an immediate personal contact, but the three who all arrived as the result of being advertised in a horse magazine, called for a more exploratory approach.

Spot was the first of these ventures, and he arrived more by lucky chance than anything else. By the time I at last saw and answered the advertisement there had already been innumerable inquiries for him, and though we were then short-listed there were still three of four families who had priority. Fortunately for us none of them proved quite suitable. Spotty had done a very special job for the family who owned him, by restoring his boy rider's nerve and setting him on the path that has since led to his becoming an eminent member of the top echelons of the Pony Club. When Spot was outgrown it was very hard to part with him, and his family's eventual decision was that the pony should go somewhere where he might "do some more good in the world". It was a happy chance for us that the Twala Club qualified.

Pinocchio and Taffy were acquired at different times, but in each case one of the advertised requirements was for a home where there was a sense of humour prevailing. And since it would be impossible to run this type of club without this particular quality, and that ponies in need of it in their riders seem to suit us, their owners and I at least started off with something in common. And this led on to the sensible mutual investigation which experience has taught us is indispensable.

## *AGREEMENTS—PRELIMINARY*

Where possible the first step is for the prospective lender and borrower to meet up and see if they like each other—an obvious aid to future good relations—and whether they share roughly the same views on looking after and riding ponies. The next steps are equally obvious: that the borrower should see and try the prospective pony, and that the lender should inspect its future home.

Too often, even such manifest safeguards are omitted without thought; occasionally circumstances prevent them. In fact, because I could not get away, neither Pinocchio nor Taffy were seen before arrival; full information was obtainable about both, however, and their owners were meticulous in their inquiries about a home for two much loved ponies. Pinocchio's owner came over to inspect our way of life and the other ponies, and brought a batch of recent photographs to convince me of his suitability for the club.

For various reasons Taffy's owner and I were restricted to getting to know each other through letters and talking on the phone. Once again my introduction to the pony was through a selection of photos. This was not the best way of setting about the deal, but Taffy's owner seemed convinced of the genuineness of our set-up, and she was as frank about her pony, "warts and all", as Pinocchio's had been. She also accompanied Taffy when he came to us, and would have been welcome to remove him if the club and what it had to offer had not been to her liking.

In both instances I made sure that the owners had addresses and phone numbers of other people who had loaned us ponies and were willing to provide references—and this is an important safeguard from the lender's point of view.

The acquisition of Briggy presented no problems because he belonged to friends of long standing, and the sad decision after some months with the club that this super little pony was too old for the job, was a mutual one. With Amber, too, reciprocal details were first conveyed by a mutual friend, making the bargain easy to arrange.

Spotty's owner and I did everything according to the book. We met, liked what we saw, and discovered we held exactly similar views about ponies and everything to do with them. She came to look at Spot's future home, and I took a club member over to try him out before making the final decision.

In Jason's case we met him and his owner at the same time, when I took two of our boys over to see what she made of their handling, and what they, as his future riders, made of the cob. The situation was a little out of the ordinary because Jason had been running out in twenty-three acres for two years, with only occasional riding, and by size and behaviour was more of a challenge than anything the club had previously encountered. He was excessively fat and it was impossible to get a saddle on him. Undeterred, the boys in turn climbed aboard bare-back to see what could be done. With the first rider Jason amiably agreed to move around at walk and trot, though owing to his

5. *New ponies sometimes mean problems—but Taffy soon agreed to co-operate.*

figure he was prone to corner broadside on, and there was a glint in his eye that I felt might present some challenges to his riders in the future. Deaf to my protests, our second boy trotted soberly up the full length of the sloping field, only to swing round and canter smartly back downhill, jumping a tree-trunk for good measure on the way. Predictably the big cob bucked on landing, but the rolls of fat kept his rider in place and totally unperturbed. Everyone seemed to be enjoying themselves, and both lender and recipient had to agree that the trio seemed well suited!

## *AGREEMENTS—ON PAPER*

When the preliminaries have proved satisfactory to both sides, but preferably before the horse or pony actually arrives in its new home, is the moment to set out on paper a friendly agreement of terms. Two copies of the document should be signed and exchanged, properly witnessed and dated; it may or may not be legally binding, but it is a sensible method of going about the transaction. And if there are any future troubles something like this can help to iron them out.

The statement should include a full description of the animal—sex, colour, size, age and name—and a list of all tack and accessories sent with it. In addition to sending back saddle and bridle, I undertake replacement of the small items that are liable to be mislaid when or if the pony is returned. There should be notes about what immunizing it has been given, when "booster" injections are due, and whether to the best of its owner's knowledge the animal is sound on the date of delivery.

It is important to state whether the animal is insured, and if so who is to be responsible for future premiums, and if a saddle and bridle are included, also the sum for which these are insured. In our case we do a "cover" insurance for the club ponies that are aged ten and under, and for the tack; but if the premium for a particular pony and its saddle and bridle is too high for club finances, the owner and I come to some amicable arrangement for sharing the cost.

Whether a loan is technically "indefinite" or not, there may well be a moment when, due to unforeseen circumstances, it has to be terminated by one side or the other, and it should be set down how much notice is required—unless an act of God makes this impossible! I like to include a promise to the owner that if anything dramatic should happen to me or to the pony, he or she will be immediately informed. I also stress that while every care is taken, I cannot be held responsible if, despite this, the animal is injured, killed, or has to be destroyed.

Some owners like to make provisos about the purposes for which their animals may be used. If these are reasonable and fit in with requirements, that is fair enough—so long as they are clearly stated, understood, and agreed on. Genuine pony-lovers will do their best to comply with all fair and sensible requests, but sometimes this proves impossible.

As a good-looking palomino, Pinocchio had been successfully shown in hand, and it was laid down that he was not to be trimmed. This was easy to agree. He looked very pretty with his flowing mane and tail, everyone was proud to have such a good-looking pony and only too happy to keep him that way. What could not be foreseen was that one night Pinocchio and Spot would indulge in that equine sport of "you scratch my neck and I'll scratch yours", a mutual grooming session that must have become frenzied. By morning we were horror-struck to find both ponies very raggedly "hogged", and there was the unenviable task of confessing to Pinocchio's owner that her palomino's beautiful lengthy mane was no more. Luckily we had managed to imbue her pony with a new interest in jumping during the weeks he had been with us and this proved some compensation for his altered appearance. To level up his looks we were then allowed to trim his heels and shorten his tail, and they are being kept that way until his mane is no longer reminiscent of a Przevalski horse.

As an illustration of unreasonable stipulations there was the time when I was very tempted to take on a couple of Connemara mares for the club. They were a most attractive, mannered pair, and their persuasive owner had almost got me to agree when she started laying down rules about what the ponies could, and principally could not, do and also exactly how much they were to be given to eat. In the end it boiled down to what amounted to a programme of light hacking for a few hours a week, and I was fortunate to discover at that stage that both were in foal. In fact the club was being asked to look after and feed two animals that were scarcely to be used until their condition prohibited riding altogether, and they were then presumably to be handed back to their opportunist owner!

On another occasion I was foolishly persuaded to accept the loan of a cob with "a leg". His young owner was perfectly genuine, but her understandable reluctance to have an old friend put down made her clutch at any straw. Unfortunately her assurances that any stiffness in his hock wore off with work proved optimistic to say the least. Work or no work the cob remained very lame, and, in the week or so that we had him, showed himself as a most unco-operative character. In this case there had been no provisos about the animal's use—but, sadly, he was useless.

Both these instances rammed home the fact that when a pony is offered on loan, it is not only the lender who has to be careful!

Experience has now taught me to ensure that any pony we take on may be used for anything reasonable that the club contemplates doing, but at a standard within the animal's scope. And if some new venture crops up, a Pony Club Camp for instance, permission from the owner is always previously sought.

Pony-owners are also always encouraged to come at intervals and visit, and ride, their own animals. Club members take pride in turning out pony and saddlery to best effect and, as they did with Pinocchio's owner, then taking their guests out for a picnic ride—quite regardless of weather.

*NUMBER OF PONIES*

If we are lucky enough to have little difficulty in acquiring ponies on loan (and usually even more lucky in their qualities and the kindness of their owners), with a club like this it is not quite as easy to decide the number of ponies that best suits the situation. In fact this is something that has to be determined through the years by trial and error, because the exact ratio of riders to ponies has to depend partly on the available cash and facilities, but also to a large extent on the ability and keenness of the members. And those are factors that are related, but vary at different stages of a club's development.

Too few ponies can be frustrating, too many can be an embarrassment to those who feel they ought to be riding when they do not particularly want to—and a source of irritation to someone like myself who does not enjoy seeing ponies not being reasonably utilized!

Our starting ratio of only a couple of ponies to ten riders, remained possible for no more than a few weeks, yet, given the rawness of those early recruits, the situation had its advantages. At the time, none of the riders had ever before had to catch and groom the pony they were taking out. True, they had been required to tack up their own mounts at the riding school, but the animals had been there awaiting them, already clean and, bar saddling, ready to go. To have to do the catching and grooming themselves was something different. Riding took on a new dimension; it required more effort, physical and mental. The interest was still there, but that absorption and almost automatic horse-sense common in families with a long-standing background of horse was, reasonably enough, totally lacking.

Now it often amazes me just how comparatively horse-minded the Twala Club families have become, but, although in each group there will usually be one or two children who are dedicated, they are all still children of their generation. For the majority, ponies are not the only interest and there is no reason why they should be. This is something I have had

6. *When the ration of riders to ponies is roughly two to one, sharing is part of club life.*

to accept and learn, just as these young people have had to assimilate the quota of horse-sense that they have now, mostly, achieved.

Another good reason why ten riders found two ponies sufficient for requirements for a while was because none of them had ever before been "out for a ride". They had been confined to an indoor school for a short period once a week, and riding off into the countryside under their own steam was a somewhat daunting, and apparently tiring, prospect. They tended to find their feet by going for very short rides, often no more than half-an-hour, and this meant that, if required, the ponies could go out several times in one day.

Eventually we graduated to four ponies for twelve riders, and this worked well for a long time. It was not until some of our original, or near original, members began to ride really well and became comparatively ambitious, that we upped the number of ponies to our limit of six.

In the club's second summer I made the mistake of accepting the temporary loan of a couple more ponies for the holidays. This made six at the time, and was far too many for the level of our enthusiasm and standards. During those holidays I seemed to spend my days rounding up, and urging on to a pony, members happy to ride two or three times a week but with small inclination to do so more or less every day.

And I remember how one of the boys who was contemplating our stud, for once all inhabiting the same field, put the situation in a nutshell. "We all love ponies," he remarked, "but this is ridiculous!"

## *Chapter Four*

# PONIES AND PONIES

HOWEVER EXCITING IT may be to find a pony on loan, however tempting the offer, it is essential to have a very clear idea of what kind of pony fits the club bill at that particular stage, and to resist taking on anything, however attractive, if it does not approximate to requirements.

There are exceptions to every rule, but in general very young ponies and anything with any appreciable "blood" are not suited to Twala Club facilities or activities. This does not mean that we require characterless "slugs"; half the fun of keeping ponies collectively is that there is an assortment to ride, each with its own idiosyncrasies and abilities. But however much our ponies vary in size, shape and temperament, as far as is possible for creatures of flesh and blood they have got to be safe, both to handle and to ride.

As time has gone by it has become possible, and desirable, to qualify slightly our interpretation of the term "safe". But bearing in mind that anyone who organizes a club of this kind is responsible for a number of other people's children and ponies, the type to be sought is that which if treated and ridden with sense, can be trusted to behave under normal circumstances. And, since reliable animals do not come two a penny, this club has been exceptionally lucky to date in the number that have qualified.

### *TWALA*

Owing to age and his feet not being quite what they were, Twala's active participation in the club was short-lived, but while it lasted it was a distinct asset.

Despite his years, he was really too big and strong for his

riders at that time, but always willing: amenable to being caught and handled, totally traffic-proof, and never one to take advantage, he proved an excellent tutor. None of his riders were then capable of appreciating the high quality of his schooling, but Twala made his own arrangements about any lack of or wrongly applied aids, and seldom put a hoof wrong. That old pony taught them many things, not least the fun attached to riding, and, whether in use or in retirement, he was the obvious choice for Club President. In that capacity he makes an annual appearance at the club show—where many admirers from the past are delighted to renew his acquaintance.

*AUNT JABISKA*

Some time before the club came into being it was obvious that Twala's working days were numbered, and I set out to find myself a successor. It seemed a modest wish to want a mannered, moderate-looking 14.2 hand pony, of an age that should more or less see out my riding days, but current prices were a shock. Eventually I settled for quite a nice 14 hand grey, and it was a worse shock to discover that when ridden solo he frequently had only one gear—and that was in reverse. It was not only I who had to acknowledge this the most nappy animal ever encountered, as he proved a match for far better horsemen than myself. After he carted me, at speed but backwards, off a track into the middle of a busy road, I decided that life was too short to have it further curtailed—and my new purchase was returned.

The grey mare suggested as a replacement looked everything I did not want. Her bony frame was supported on thick and very hairy legs, she was goose-rumped to excess at one end, and her poor, thin neck could scarcely support a large plain head at the other. There was an ugly cut behind her ears that made her flinch when approached, and it was apparent that she was in a bad state of malnutrition. But she looked at me with big, pleading eyes, and when I mounted and asked for the few yards at walk and trot of which she seemed capable, she tried to

7. *Aunt Jabiska taught them everything, including how to showjump.*

arch her travesty of a neck with pride, and responded to the slightest aid.

Jabiska was never exactly a beauty, but after six weeks' running out in a neighbour's twenty-acre pasture she was unrecognizable as the poor, ugly creature I had bought. She also turned out to be a pleasant, willing hack for myself, and the most perfect animal that could have been found for the early days of a set-up like the Twala Club.

Gentle and kind, the mare took it upon herself to look after her riders to a degree that was remarkable. There was no need for qualms when even the most inefficient was riding her, and she quite literally taught them how to go for country hacks—never attempting to turn and make for home, or change gear unless asked and, while willing and happy to canter on if required, steadying or stopping without hesitation. It was Jabiska who escorted ponies and riders to their first, very elementary gymkhanas, and she who was chiefly responsible for showing the members how to hop safely over small obstacles or play gymkhana games.

In those days, as now, the more experienced riders were expected to help the lesser fry—even if it was largely a matter of the blind leading the blind. Some of the "helping", though full of good intentions, was not really according to British Horse Society ideas—as I discovered one day on congratulating a member for having mastered the art of cantering, and being then told of the method employed.

This was for a helper, on foot, to accompany Jabiska and rider to a stretch of nearby tow-path. The helper than sat at ease in the grass, while the rider trotted off for a quarter of a mile or so, flipped the mare round, gave her a slap and belted back to his companion. The routine was repeated six or seven times for a few evenings, until that particular rider had got the rhythm correctly—and never once did the grey mare refuse to play her part, or go much faster than was intended, or attempt to slip past the "finishing post" and make for home.

However, no one is quite perfect, and Jabiska's allergy to

midges proved a stumbling-block until a remedy was discovered. Her nose was obviously extremely sensitive to the attacks of these pests and at times in summer she became almost unrideable, charging along with her head stuck up in the air like an inebriated giraffe, or scraping her nostrils along the road. Nothing that vet or chemist could produce had the slightest effect, and we were in despair until I came on one of those fringe contraptions, normally attached to the brow-band of a head-collar to keep flies away from the eyes of grazing ponies.

Jabiska wore hers attached to her nose-band, where the plastic strips hung down, covering nose and mouth. She nibbled it a bit at first, but it worked like a dream and became an integral part of the mare's summer wear. And if it did look a little unusual, even the judges at local gymkhanas became used to the sight of Aunt Jabiska's "slipped yashmak".

Her violent aversion to vets also caught me by surprise, but was no doubt due to rough treatment at some time in her obscure past. With one exception, she was in fact always a little wary of males and could lead the boys a dance if she had no mind to be caught—particularly the unhorse-minded young man who once set out to capture her when wearing full PVC motor-bike gear that flapped and crackled in the wind. The girls had only to go into the field, tell Jabiska that she really was lovely, and the mare would stand motionless, fluttering her eyelashes. But she would come to call for the boy she loved.

This was an older member, one of the originals, to whom the art of riding did not come easily. During the sessions at the riding school he had appeared to spend an appreciable part of the time on the tan-covered floor rather than on his horse. Like Jabiska he, too, was gentle by nature and a bit of a loner, and they proved kindred spirits with a rare affection for each other. On warm summer evenings it was a familiar sight to see Jabiska lying down and her friend, seated between her folded legs, leaning back against her side while he talked to her. They went for long country rambles together, and eventually became quite successful partners in the first little novice cross-country competitions attempted by the club.

Jabiska had been with us for about two years when I was riding her one day and she stumbled and pitched down on to her nose. We were on grass and there was no harm done, but it was worrying when the same thing happened during a club class. Twice more and it was time to call the vet. The results of the X-ray were not encouraging. Jabiska had navicular disease and pedal osteitis, and we tried all the usual shoeing and other alleviations, including eventually partial de-nerving. For six weeks after that operation the mare could not have been happier and was obviously free from all pain. Then she was seen again shuffling from foot to foot in the field, and even resting one front hoof on top of the other. With no more to be done to relieve the pain, we had no option but to have her put down. It was a very sad decision to make—and there was one member of the club whose enthusiasm for riding vanished almost overnight.

*SPOTTY*

Registered as Tiger Tim, but re-christened for his spotty coat, this 12.3 hand, well-moving little Welsh pony (Section B) was an acquisition that first belonged to, but long outlived, the Jabiska era. He was a great character, very well schooled but with a mind of his own, and possessed of the most expressive face of any pony I have seen.

It was an unforgettable incident meeting up with him at a gymkhana when one of our club mothers, trying out her increasing grasp of horse-sense, had offered to take charge of Spot when he was not competing. Quite correctly she had loosened his girth, run up the stirrups, and pulled the reins over his head. But for some reason she was walking out in front of the pony, her hands clasped behind her back. Spotty was trudging along astern, his saddle, unnoticed, slung beneath his stomach, his eyes rolling, his nose wrinkled up with disgust, and most patently muttering "Women. . . !" under his breath.

For his first week with the club, Spot's manners remained impeccable and a tribute to his owner. But by the end of that time he had gauged the depths of his new riders' inexperience and, in the manner of the majority of his kind, set out to exploit the situation. Soon the air in the schooling field began to ring with despairing shouts of "Spotty!", as he carted his riders in turn back to the gate or side-tracked the 12″ pole he was supposed to be jumping. He was foolproof on the road and normally behaved well when out in company. Taken out by himself around the countryside he was not above stopping, waiting to see what the reactions might be and, if the response was feeble, then swinging round and making for home, urged on as he thought by a rider crouched hopelessly up his neck.

I began to detect muttered references amongst the girls to "Horrid Spotty . . !", but, after delivering a withering broadside to the effect that it was more a case of "Stupid, ineffectual riders . . !", plugged home with some forceful advice about mastering one's mount, was relieved to see the situation change dramatically. In the shortest time Spot capitulated and reverted to his former mannered self, and quickly became the most popular pony with all those of a size to ride him.

*PAINT*

Jabiska's loss left a big and much lamented hole in the club ranks, but before it occurred we were lucky to have taken on Paint—the stocky, 14 hand piebald that my eldest daughter had been riding in Devon, until her capabilities outstripped his.

Immediately before coming to us, Paint had spent a year at a riding school where much of the tuition takes place on the wide open spaces of Dartmoor, and this spell had furthered his virtues as an enjoyable hack. Within his limits, at that time considerably higher than those of the Twala Club members, the pony was also an honest competitor in novice show-jumping and hunter trials and, although game, was always comfortingly one-hundred-per-cent safe—invaluable as a mount for any new entry to the club. But now, at eighteen, more than minimal jumping in a club class has become a bit of an effort, and he is seldom used for competing. Unfortunately club finances necessitate every pony being worth its keep and physically able to cope with all our activities, and Paint will soon be retired. But there is a happy home lined up for him where the work will be more suited to his years, and will include riding for the disabled.

*AMBER*

Until I had the luck to meet this sturdy little Exmoor, with his huge eyes and appealing face, I was sceptical of there being what is so often advertised as "a perfect pony for a child". But here is a character who never tires, normally goes where required at what speed he is asked, can jump anything up to and including a 14.2 course, and gallops round hunter trials with the same ease and enjoyment.

With the right rider Amber can produce an impressive dressage test for an animal of his type and size. He never hots

8. *Amber is exactly the right size and temperament for the smaller members.*

up or is "silly", and catches the eye with his true, native-bred good looks. He has been known to decant his rider by bucking before the start of a cross-country, but that is sheer *joie de vivre* at the thought of what is to come, and those with the good fortune to compete with him learn to sit tight at that point. He takes hold a little out hunting but knows the job inside out, is never out of control as such, and is guaranteed to give his partner maximum enjoyment.

### *FIDDLER*

When someone rang up and offered me the loan of a four-year-old for the club to have the use of for a year, my immediate reaction was that it would not be sensible, from the pony's point of view as much as his riders', to accept such a young and perforce inexperienced animal. I was still dubious even when assured that my fears could be discounted so far as this particular pony was concerned. But I was overruled, and Fiddler duly arrived.

This pony's honest, amiable outlook on life is written all over his white face, and with the good conformation of his iron-grey body, when he is in summer coat and trimmed and plaited he is a good-looking animal. He stands, now at seven years old, 14.2½ hands in his shoes, and is possibly either seven-eighths Connemara with perhaps a dash of Highland, or maybe mostly Highland with something added to make him more of a lightweight.

Owing to his tender years and because, although well broken and schooled Fiddler had obviously not done over-much, for that year we erred on the side of caution in what we asked of him. He was jumped a little at home and showed a taste for it to match his aptitude, but his activities at the few small shows he attended were confined to a go at the "clear round", a few gymkhana games, and a working pony class or two. The better riders hacked him around the countryside, and found him imperturbable to the open sea, swans flying, tractors and motor-bikes, gunfire, and even a train thundering overhead during an

9. *Fiddler is not fast, but he and his rider save time by turning quickly towards the next fence.*

inadvertent short cut through a farmer's tunnel under the railway.

By the time Fiddler's year was nearly up I knew beyond doubt that this was a super pony and exactly the one for me, as well as for the club. The problem was how to buy an animal that was way beyond my monetary reach, without even thinking about that of the club.

Not for the first time, fate came to my aid. Fiddler's owner was willing to take a low price from a home where she felt the pony fitted in so well, and out of the blue someone who knew what this pony meant to me bought him for me. It was a wonderful present.

*BRIGGY*

It was a sad moment when we had to acknowledge that "The Brigadier" was just too old for the job. A Welshman, with the typical "look of eagles", he rode bigger than his 13.1 hands and more like a horse, and was always a super, energetic hack and an enthusiastic jumper. In a riding class he showed himself off to advantage, could be guaranteed never to go on the wrong leg and went all out to catch the judges' eye; it was a wonderful experience for our riders to have a pony so permanently on his toes. But the trouble with Briggy was that he could never take life very calmly, and at nearly twenty demanded too much of himself and was just too old to stand up to club activities during the holidays.

Now his owners have found him a home with a young family, where the light work should suit him well for many years to come.

*JASON*

Something on the lines of a Welsh cob became a club necessity when the boy members persisted in growing. They also required something that would present a challenge and Jason, at 15.1 hands and having spent the formative years between five and seven doing relatively nothing, fitted the bill on both counts. As I have already said, he was enormously, grossly fat, and he spent his first week with us shut in the hunter-'chaser's stable, with a bucket of water, a very small hay-net and a little bran for company. Within two days it was possible to get a saddle on him and he was then given walking exercise. Directly his dimensions were comparatively reasonable he was turned out into one of our smaller fields, where the scanty summer grazing combined with normal club activities continued the good work. Once the fat was off him and his summer coat through, Jason emerged as a handsome, heavyweight cob in an eye-catching shade of palomino gold.

After a year in our company Jason has retained his reputation as a good, energetic hack, and grazing in fields alongside the road where lorries and tractors trundle to and fro has restored his nerve in traffic. Up to his coming I would not have contemplated taking on anything that was not one-hundred-per-cent traffic-proof, but some of our riders are now capable of coping with a few "ifs and buts", and until we were sure of him the cob was only ridden out in company and given the inside place on the road.

He has always been well-meaning and it says much for his temperament that he has calmed down as much as he has in the hands of the very inexpert. The chief trouble with him is that he is so strong. Until the day the blacksmith put the head-collar rope round Jason's nose and then round a telegraph-pole it was impossible to tie him anywhere. Fences and head-collars suffered alike, while he went where he wished. And as our ponies are usually shod out of doors, when he became bored with the shoeing process he just wandered off, trailing the "holder", the long-suffering blacksmith and his tools following along behind. He now lunges reasonably, and this is of course paying off in making him more obedient and supple, and rhythmic in his trot, and it is a far cry from the days when I was dragged about on the end of a lunge-rein all over the field. He can now be ridden out by all but the real novices, and the boys can control him hunting and take him round a novice course of show-jumps or a hunter trial. Eventing is now more than a remote possibility. Strangely enough, despite his size, he has always enjoyed and been quite good at gymkhana games. But Jason's chief mission in life, and one that he performs admirably, is to give our boy members something to "get their teeth into". Girls will remain happy for years with something to ride, and look after, and love, but boys become bored and lose interest without a mount to test their skills and against which they can pit their wits. If funds were unlimited they might dream of having a super, perfectly schooled horse with which they could conceivably win and win again. But coming back to earth they are willing to acknowledge that one little

10. *Pinocchio is a gentleman of character—but invaluable for his one hundred per cent reliability.*

rosette won with Jason represents so much effort that, in a different way, it is almost more worth while!

### *PINOCCHIO*

In his own curious way this palomino is as much of a challenge as Jason. He was bought by his owner after he had spent some years in a riding school, and although she had cured much of his sourness before he came to us, most of his remaining foibles date back to that era.

He is an amusing, sometimes exasperating, character—invaluable in a club like this. For whether Pinocchio is having an "on" or an "off" day, whether he is hacking, hunting or competing, he is two-hundred-per-cent safe however incompetent his rider.

Not that competence is always the criterion that decides Pinocchio's behaviour. Of equal importance is whether he is on good terms with his rider, and what mood he happens to be in. If all is right with his world this pony can jump 3′ 6″ over coloured fences or across country, prove a pleasant hack in company and a safe one on his own, go well in a class under instruction, and perform adequately, if without particular enthusiasm, to give a novice an enjoyable introduction to hunting.

If he is in a "mood", Pinocchio will not lift a hoof at a jump, either at home or in a competition, and can be impossible to get into a canter, even with hounds. Years of heel-drumming at the riding school have deadened his sides so that he is largely insensitive to normal aids, and use of the whip can make him more mulish. He goes best for the long-legged rider, or those sufficiently proficient to use spurs lightly and correctly, or dispense with their stirrups, and best of all for those who also love him. He tends to greet people with flattened ears and a "snarky" expression, but this is a front—put your arms round his neck and hug him and the picture alters to one of pricked ears and a pleased look in his eye.

In fact Pinocchio is one of our success stories. His moods are becoming less frequent, his abilities more to the fore and, as his owner appreciates, there is no doubt that the pony is happy and enjoying the different aspects of the Twala Club.

### *TAFFY*

This fast, tough Welsh pony, cob type (Section C), is the kind of animal that provides a yardstick of the Twala Club's progress. A year or so ago he would have so outclassed his riders that it would have been madness to take him on. Not that there is anything wrong with Taffy—he is the most super, indefatigable ride imaginable and an excellent all-rounder—but he does love to gallop on, with exceptional speed for one of his breeding, and trying to steady him at his fences can present a problem to the uninitiated. Steady him too much and he stops. But the three who ride Taffy are now not in the least afraid of the sort of galloping and jumping they have never encountered before, and in the comparatively short time since he arrived the pony, in the manner of his kind, is already starting to co-operate. There is no doubt that within a year we shall have not only what is already apparent, the pony that everyone given the privilege loves to ride, but a winning combination that is going to boost morale and prove very rewarding. Again the luck is with us.

The quality of a club like this depends largely on the quality of the ponies it keeps, combined with the outlook of the club members and those responsible for running it. And if, as I feel, the ambition should be to go forward, always to set the sights a

11. *The arrival of Taffy, clipped out and corned up, was a challenge for everyone.*

little higher, then as the years go by the type of pony required must alter to a degree. Such a club does not cater only for the better riders and there must be ponies to suit all abilities, but even the less able can be taught to ride slightly more "goey" ponies, and the more skilled can be "stretched" to cope with a few problems, and aim to improve the potential of all the animals they ride.

If all the club ponies were much of a muchness and quiet to the point of dullness, then it would be very easy for an enterprise like this to trundle along on such a low plane that there would be no room for any aspirations, however modest, and none would ever improve. To my mind there has to be incentive to breed continuing interest and if the luck is in, sufficient results at differing standards to generate yet more ambition.

The sort of ponies to make all this possible are the types that people have been kind enough to lend us. We know the club could never keep "blood" animals and there is no place for crazy ones; but equally "slugs" would never meet the bill. We need the accomplishment and potential of the Fiddlers and Ambers, the Pinocchios and Jasons and Taffys—and that is what, by good fortune, we have got.

## *Chapter Five*

# RULES AND REGULATIONS

RULES ARE OF little use unless they are kept, and the more there are, the more there are to ignore or break. We have therefore tried to keep Twala Club regulations to a minimum, but at the same time bearing in mind that the safety and well-being of both riders and ponies must depend on some stringent guide-lines, implicit if not actually defined in writing. And the same approach applies to the running of the club as a club, if it is not to degenerate into a collection of individuals each intent on getting as much out of it as possible without reference to anyone else.

Until its sixth year the club did not aspire to a rule book, as such, but one was then written for the benefit of newcomers and as a "refresher" for the old hands. It was kept as brief as possible, and was compiled from what had been learned, re-learned, added to, subtracted from and altered as necessary through the years.

These written rules are outlined in this chapter, but the bulk of what members are expected to observe still remains more by inference than by being laid down in a text—and with all our regulations the modifying process continues as situations arise and dictate.

### *AGE*

Starting from scratch, in the early days one of the first things to be decided was the age group for which the club could cater.

Now that the majority of our riders have outgrown small ponies and need something at least about 13.3 hands, the age for joining the club is not quite as elastic as it used to be. Again there is the occasional exception, but as a general rule newcomers must be at least eleven years old. Thirteen seems to be the most popular and in some ways the easiest age for membership. Children under eleven are normally too much of a liability in a club where the members are not permanently supervised.

No definite age for leaving has ever been decided because the circumstances of growing up normally determine this as a natural sequence of events. There are exceptions: now and again a "leaver" later asks to be reinstated, but usually at about sixteen young people are either embroiled in exams and temporary holiday jobs, or leave school to start work in earnest. And around this age is when other interests, usually the opposite sex and often involving motorbikes, most frequently take over, at least to some extent, from the ponies. With the boys, size and weight can also be a limiting factor to their club riding years. Jason is the only one of our animals up to any appreciable weight, and the club cannot cope with the feeding and space requirements of more than one pony over 14.2 hands, let alone anything larger than the cob.

*ASSOCIATES*

One or two who could not remain as full-time members as they grew up, asked to continue on a part-time basis. They ride at intervals, so long as a pony is available, and pay a small fee for the privilege instead of any weekly subscription. They are also expected to clean their tack afterwards, and pick up a bag of dung!

Our three "Friends of the Club" are variations on the theme of associates. One is a former member and all three have their own ponies. They come for instruction, for which they pay the fee, and join in as many club activities as they can.

*QUALIFICATIONS*

In the early days there was no regular instructor, but various good friends did a little teaching as and when they could. As the original members were those who had been attending the riding school, they did at very least know the basics, and this evolved into a policy for future newcomers.

Nowadays we are lucky enough to have a regular qualified instructor, but she comes at most once a week. Apart from these lessons the riding is unsupervised, and since the more experienced members are expected to take turns in accompanying the novices, it would be unfair, and unwise, to give these young people the responsibility of looking after complete beginners. If such riders were included in the classes they could not help impeding the instruction of the more advanced, and as all the old hands have improved, so the ponies are expected to do more and thus become less suited to the totally uninitiated.

For these reasons no one is accepted for club membership until they have attended a reputable riding school for a while, where the teaching is on similar lines to our own. The number of lessons depends on their own ability, but before joining the club they have to be reasonably safe at walk and trot, to have embarked on cantering and, most important of all, be capable of stopping any reasonably well-behaved pony!

For the first week or two after becoming members and until considered ready to venture into the outside world, newcomers are confined to riding in the schooling field—under the guidance of a more experienced rider. And until promoted, strictly on merit, they are restricted to riding ponies with the understanding qualities of Paint, Pinocchio or Amber.

## *PARENTAL INVOLVEMENT*

Another important qualification of membership is that the parents of any would-be members must understand and accept that they themselves will be expected to "muck in" and play their part in all club activities, including the weekly hay-feeding rota in winter. Some parents prove better at raising the wind financially than erecting a barbed wire fence, but there is room for all talents—and it is the spirit that counts!

## *ON PROBATION*

Because an adequate rider does not necessarily make a good club member, newcomers are given an unofficial probationary period of two months. To date, although an occasional warning has been necessary, no one has failed to make the grade—although a persistent breaker of rules, regardless of how long he or she has been a member, may be asked to leave.

## *DRESS*

So long as the obligatory hard hat and "sensible" low-heeled shoes or other appropriate footwear are worn, the everyday garb of the Twala Club is much the same as it was in the beginning—the ubiquitous jeans worn with a shirt or jersey, and an anorak for cold weather. And before they accede to any pleas for other "proper" riding kit, parents of newcomers are strongly advised to wait a while and make sure their child's wish to ride and join the club is not a passing phase.

Twice in the past, a new member has appeared after only a

12. *The club parents, horseminded or not, are always willing helpers. Boxing Pinocchio with the aid of lunge reins.*

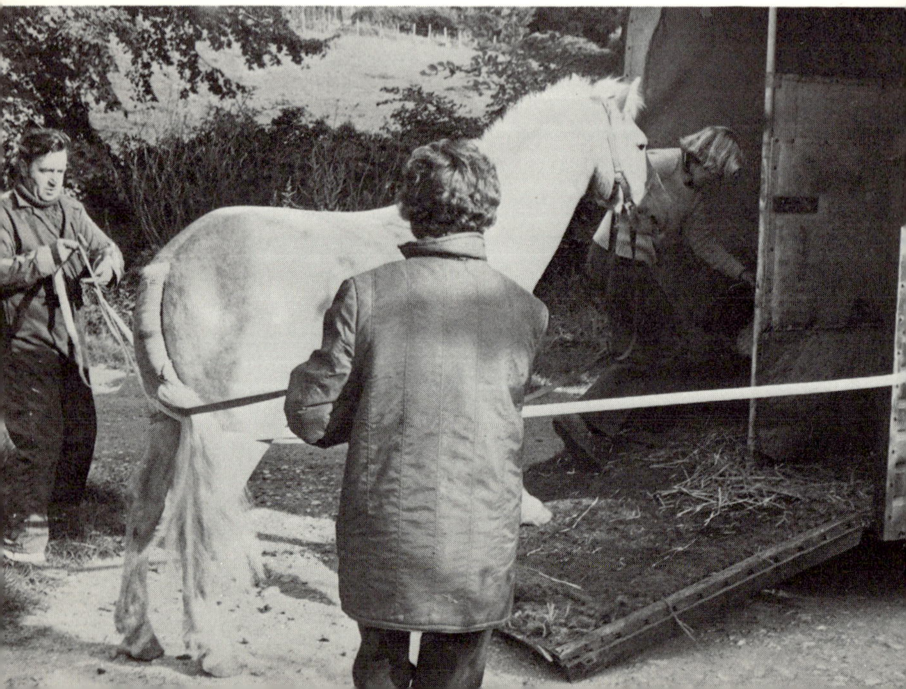

week or so decked out in all the correct gear. One, a girl, was suspected of being more interested in "looking pretty on a horse" than in all the inevitable chores connected with the beasts. Her quickly waning enthusiasm disappeared altogether after an unfortunate fall. The other, a boy, was athletically-minded and enjoyed the riding but disinclined for dirty work. In both cases it seemed a pity that the parents had been put to unnecessary expense.

Nowadays our members take pride in being neatly turned out, and appear in public with themselves and their ponies looking a real credit to the club. And it was pleasant to be rung up by a lady, renowned for somewhat jaundiced views on modern young riders and their dress, to be told that she had just passed a Twala Club contingent returning from a show who, by clothes and behaviour, were quite obviously "real horsemen".

In the old days the club owned a number of donated riding hats and other apparel that regularly went the rounds. Some of it had already done yeoman service with my own family, including one notable riding hat that, for obvious reasons, was known as the "blancmange". There was also a very smart tailor-made blue coat. Given to my daughters years ago, it then, until outgrown by everyone, regularly appeared adorning the backs of different Twala Club members, in different classes at the same show—to the amusement of those who watched the change-over.

Now, after the probation period, everyone manages to get themselves very smartly equipped, even down to the girls' hair-nets—items of incredulous controversy when first introduced by their instructor, but now accepted as normal correct wear for correct occasions.

### *SAFETY*

Obviously the rules concerning this subject are those most rigorously enforced, and all the normal safety measures are taken. But it is impossible to cater for all eventualities, such as the day one of our members and her pony were attacked by a young stallion that was tethered but up-ended its picket-pin on sight of them.

She was riding on a common that is anyway out of bounds, but, instead of scarpering back home directly she had managed to get away from the animal, she decided to be public-spirited and inform the police. On returning to the scene with a police officer she was promptly attacked again at which point she baled out, and pony and stallion took off round the town. Fortunately both were caught without any ill effects to anyone, but there are no rules, written or implied, to cover a situation like that.

### *HATS AND WAISTCOATS*

The important rule, that no one is allowed to get on a pony's back without their riding-cap, is one always enforced—and, to the best of my knowledge, always abided by.

The club has also been given orange "fluorescent" waistcoats, and they have to be used for the purpose for which they are intended, that is for riding in poor light. Gone are the days when a white-faced pony at the head of a contingent and a white-tailed one bringing up the rear after dark provided sufficient warning to the occasional car. Nowadays the traffic even on country lanes calls for something on the lines of those excellent garments. The Twala Club are supposed to be back home before dark, but if they do happen to get benighted, or are abroad on a murky winter's afternoon, these waistcoats, carried in a pocket, can be donned and the riders are then easily distinguishable from quite a distance.

### *"OUTSIDERS"*

One of the first rules was, and to a degree still is, the most difficult to observe. This is that no one outside the club may ride any of the ponies, or be given a ride on one, without special permission first being obtained. It seemed a harsh regulation, but there are good reasons for it.

In the early days the local lads' immediate reaction to seeing one of their mates doing anything so outlandish as riding a horse, was to roar with laughter, throw stones at the animal's legs, and do their best to make it shy. When that palled they demanded to be allowed "to have a go"! And to some extent this still happens, particularly with the newer recruits when first promoted to riding out on their own.

It is not easy to say "no" to a friend, but the request has to be resisted as it could be unsafe for both rider and pony, and because only club members are covered for third-party risks by our insurance policy.

The rule is also applied to members when riding with friends who are outside the club. Again a difficult one when it is tempting to change ponies, but enforced for the same reasons. Another is that our ponies are all schooled on the same lines, which may not be those of the "friend", and could be confused by strange riders.

### *FIELD REGULATIONS*

Another tough rule, enforced in the name of safety, is that excluding from our fields any child who is not a member, even if he or she happens to be a younger brother or sister anxious to "help" with the ponies. Few understood the reasons for this one until the day a small boy was in amongst four ponies milling about by the gate. He was only trying to pat one of them, but inevitably they had food in mind and started to charge around kicking at each other. The luck was with us and the child was extracted undamaged, but it was an effective, and frightening, lesson.

### *BOOKING RIDERS*

Through the years a variety of methods have been tried out to ensure that everyone gets their fair share of riding, and the ponies their fair share of exercise.

No system has proved infallible, but the most successful to date is to keep a large diary in the tack-room. The dates of lessons, shows, etc. are entered in advance, plus the day of rest that each pony earns automatically after competing. Otherwise riders book the pony they want about a week beforehand. There are, however, two provisos connected with this that are not always observed.

If a member cannot ride on that particular day, he is supposed to cancel the booking in the diary—so that someone else can. In theory all members are also supposed to look back to check that the pony they want does in fact need exercising as much as any of the others. Fortunately the diary enables me to check such information as this for myself, and I can make the necessary adjustments at the times when one or two ponies are suffering from an excess of popularity—with others much in need of being ridden.

Another diary rule that is not always implemented is that no one, except myself, writes anything in it that is not strictly "booking business". As it is, the diary can make amusing reading, and the messages it contains are usually indicative of the emotional state of the club!

## *PONIES' WORK TIMES*

In the terms when there is sufficient light in the evening, the ponies are usually ridden for a while after school as well as at weekends. During winter evenings they get little but weekend work.

Club work is seldom exacting, although on Saturdays and Sundays and during the school holidays they are normally ridden most days and sometimes twice a day. When this occurs the number of hours they normally work in any one day must not exceed four, with a two-hour rest-break between rides, and if the work warrants it each pony has one day off per week.

In the summer all-day riding picnics are a popular pastime, but one for which permission has to be obtained. The group carry their food in knapsacks, and the ponies wear head-collars under their bridles, the tying-ropes round their necks. They are restricted on mileage and a good midway rest for man and beast is obligatory, during which the ponies are watered and tied where they can browse or graze. The tying-up was enforced after I assured members that so long as they were on the tow-path, with a closed gate between them and home, the ponies could graze free—and Paint promptly let me down by instigating a three-mile stampede in the opposite direction.

### *CONSIDERATION*

An understanding of how much a pony can take—and the realization that this varies as much with different ponies as it does with different people—is all part of the embracing subject known as horse-sense. The old hands of the Twala Club can still make mistakes, but by and large they can now assess, without thinking, how much fast work is enough, or when to call a halt to the schooling over jumps that is proving such fun for the rider. They now know that if a pony of Taffy's temperament were to show signs of tiredness he would be very tired indeed—but that if Pinocchio intimated the same thing he would more probably be "trying it on". Usually they err on the side of too little work rather than too much, but that is a good fault, and with each day that passes they become more experienced, more considerate of what is good for the pony instead of only what is good entertainment for themselves.

But it has to be remembered that while the majority of the club members have now acquired varying degrees of horse-sense, often newcomers have none, and can be quite unintentionally thoughtless.

The danger moment often comes when the new member has surmounted the first few hurdles and is promoted to riding alone or schooling in the field by himself. That is the time when a pony could be found to have been taken for a nine-mile hack on the day before a competition, or if may be discovered that a rider, flushed with her own success at jumping, has been hard at it for the past hour. The rules may have been explained, but they are relatively meaningless until the reason for their being made is intelligently understood.

This kind of thing does not happen very often and most newcomers are soon on the road to becoming old hands, but it should be borne in mind that there are a great number of people in the world to whom it just does not occur that a horse or pony is anything more than a hairy, flesh-and-blood kind of machine.

### *TACK CLEANING*

To look after tack properly, and have it looking as it should, is a component of the real horseman, but, like horse-sense, is an outlook that is seldom inborn.

As with most of the club chores, various rota systems for cleaning tack have been tried, with none of them entirely successful. It seems that there will always be the conscientious few who clean their saddle and bridle properly as a matter of course, those who clean it with apparently little or no effect, and those who will always get out of cleaning it if they possibly can.

These last are in the minority, but as usual it is unfair on the faithful "willing horses". And, in addition to the fact that tack *has* to be cleaned if it is to last and be a credit to the pony it adorns, there is a cogent reason for club tack being kept properly. Just as the ponies are on loan, and therefore in trust to us, so has the club been entrusted with their often valuable tack, and both have therefore to be treated with more than ordinary care.

Usually, with time, it dawns on even the least scrupulous that regular tack cleaning makes the chore much easier. And to hasten that outlook a new regulation is now in force. Anyone who misses out on tack cleaning when they come in from a ride is stood off riding for a week; two omissions carry the penalty of a riderless two weeks; three, a month. At the moment the threat is proving effective—and it has not been necessary to consider what happens after that!

### *MANNERS, AND COUNTRY AND FARMING LORE*

The atmosphere between horse-riders and the rest of the world is not always as honeyed as it might be when they meet up on the roads, or encroach on each other's preserves around the countryside. This seems both a pity and to a large extent

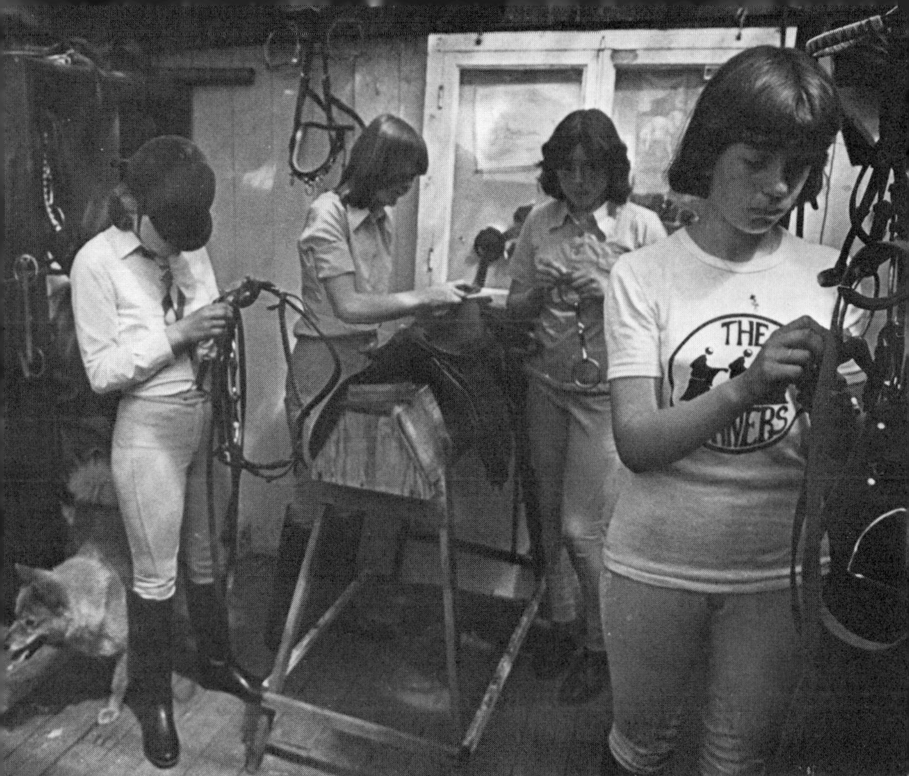


13. *The Twala club takes justifiable pride in its tack-room—and that does inspire good tack cleaning.*

unnecessary, and the Twala Club is expected to play its part, however small that may be, towards peaceful coexistence.

Members are taught to smile at and thank the car and lorry drivers who do slow down, to refrain from showing off by bounding around in public places, and to appreciate that no pedestrian likes being passed at speed, old people and young children in particular. The majority have learned from experience that to pass by a dog at anything faster than a walk, invites it to snap and bark at the pony's heels.

Our riders are taught to show courtesy to the fishermen who

enjoy their sport along the banks of the canal, and to keep off tow-paths and foot-paths alike when these are wet and muddy underfoot and liable to be further churned up by the ponies' hooves. In our district, so long as this kind of common sense and consideration is observed, equines are not expected to remain solely on the few bridle-paths, so that virtue brings its own reward!

The same outlook is encouraged towards the farmers and their land. If a rider shuts all gates and secures them as he found them, never gets above a walk where there is stock, keeps off ploughed land and stubble that may be sown or undersown, and asks permission before using a farm-track, then succeeding riders of equal consideration will usually be made welcome.

We get few complaints, but if there is one it is thoroughly investigated. Until attractive club badges were fabricated by a club father to be worn on the side of a brow-band, we were sometimes landed with the transgressions of a couple of ponies in the district who bear a strong resemblance to two of ours. Now this mistake cannot occur, but our badges do work both ways. If anyone does transgress, the blame inevitably comes home to roost.

## *MISCELLANEOUS*

So much comes under this heading, but whether it is included as actual regulations or as ingredients of common and horse sense, is a matter of opinion.

It concerns such items as removing as much mud as possible from a pony before going out for a ride—unless it is wet, when cleanliness can be abandoned except for under saddle and girth. Feet have to be picked out before setting forth, and worn shoes and risen clenches reported. Tack must also be examined for wear and tear when it is being cleaned. Any untoward incidents concerning pony or rider have always to be recounted, however trivial they may appear at the time, or however foolish the rider may be feeling.

It was a shamefaced member who confessed to letting go of

Briggy, and a friend's pony, when their riders dismounted to adjust a saddle, and some flying swans startled the ponies. Both galloped off but were retrieved without harm—except to Briggy's nerves with regard to swans. If the incident had not been reported, some less experienced rider might have been caught unawares, and with a less harmless outcome, when the pony met the same hazard in the future.

The unwritten rules may concede that it is impossible to bring in an unclipped pony dry, but insist that it should at least be brought in cool, and rubbed down with straw before being turned out to roll and strap itself. And for all their inclination to set off on a ride at speed, in the tradition of all the best cowboy movies, riders are expected to walk the first half-mile to settle their mounts, physically and mentally, for what is to come.

In fact, walking seems to be a frequent bone of contention. With a few exceptions, most tend to forget or ignore that ponies are creatures of habit, and that if they are allowed to drool along when being led, no one can blame them if they wish to move in the same manner when being ridden.

There are rules governing feeding and competing, but they are contained in the chapters given over to those absorbing subjects. Otherwise the remainder cover such matters as anyone who puts a pony away after riding being automatically responsible for checking the water. And since Spot is not the only pony adept at escaping, all gates or hurdles have to be tied securely at the bottom as well as at the top. After attempting to retrieve an unco-operative Pinocchio from someone's lawn, under the eye of the owner, this is a rule liable to be observed by at least two club members.

### *MEETINGS*

Rules—written, unwritten, observed or not—like any other relevant subject are always open to discussion at the club meetings, which average six a year. And these are the times when parents and members alike are expected to attend if

14. *Fathers, mothers, members and ponies always enjoy a good get-together. Celebrating the completion of the shelter complex.*

possible and air their views on all aspects of the club. Members occasionally hold an unofficial meeting on their own, occasions when they can hold forth on subjects they do not always want to bring up at the general meetings but opinions on which can be passed on to the right quarters. And, since an association like the Twala Club is run solely for its young members, the more they have to say and discuss about everything to do with it, the better.

## *Chapter Six*

# MONEY MATTERS—MAKING IT

WHEN WRITING ABOUT something like the Twala Club it is not always easy to determine exactly which horse should go before which cart, but as the cost of keeping ponies was one of the reasons for forming the club, and there could be no club without the money to run it, the financial side can scarcely be left until last.

### *ADMINISTRATION*

The club has only two "official" officials, the Chairman and the Treasurer. The latter's vital office usually lasts two years and is undertaken by one or another of the members' fathers. Apart from spraying fields and helping with anything and everything else, his principal tasks are to provide twice-yearly statistics bearing out just what expensive creatures ponies are, and to pay the bills and supply the second signature required on our cheques. His most important and almost impossible undertaking is that of containing my ambitions for the club and its members, four-legged as well as two, somewhere within our shoe-string financial limits.

Someone once remarked to a mutual friend that whoever ran the Twala Club must make "quite a good thing financially" out of it—a suggestion that has passed into club history as the joke of the century. But to be serious, even in the unlikely event of a similar scheme actually making money, to my mind there should be no question of anyone trying to run such a venture at a personal profit. Somehow the Twala Club has to be self-supporting. For peace of mind, in addition to funds to meet running expenses, there must be sufficient in hand to cope with the occasional out-of-the-blue outlay. It would be pleasant to have some regular source of income over and above what we manage to make for ourselves in what is perforce a hand-to-mouth existence. But there are always a hundred and one new ventures that such a club could embark on, given the money, and these would swallow up at a gulp any sum the operator might conceivably look upon as a legitimate profit for himself!

The club finances are based on the weekly subscriptions that the Treasurer keeps as petty cash to meet a variety of transactions, including such items as payment for the blacksmith, and buying anything from fencing-staples to Jason's cod-liver oil. There is a current banking account, normally down to rock-bottom by the end of spring but, optimistically, during the rest of the year sufficient to meet the remainder of the usual bills. A small emergency fund is invested with a building society to accrue interest until needed.

And considering all things, our financial crises, although blooming annually like the flowers, have so far not been too drastic. Our worst year was the one when, in a matter of weeks, the tree of Paint's saddle collapsed, the imperturbable Fiddler suffered sudden claustrophobia and stripped the inside of a good friend's trailer, Jason and Pinocchio both needed the vet, our unspeakable climate necessitated feeding all the ponies on winter rations well into the month of May, and someone stole four head-collars. Even with that lot the club still managed to retain some sort of reserve.

### *SUBSCRIPTIONS*

When riding lessons were being sponsored in the pre-club days, the recipients were still asked to contribute a token sum towards their tuition. This was not expected by our generous sponsors, but was initiated because psychologically it helped to make the lessons more appreciated than if they were entirely for free.

When the club was formed, the policy was, as it has remained, to fix the weekly subscription at the minimum—the main reason being to ensure that there would be no risk of losing, for financial reasons, any of the members for whom the club is of most benefit. And for a while, when the demands on the two or three ponies then involved were relatively light and expenses therefore matched up, club finances were met principally by donations from "outside", given by friends sufficiently interested in the scheme to wish to further it.

Even now we get the occasional generous donation, by good fortune usually turning up when most needed, but, apart from such windfalls, after the first year the club had to pay its own way to survive. As the years go by and inflation continues to bite—while the riders get better and more ambitious and the ponies have to come in larger sizes—this becomes increasingly difficult; so far, however, with maximum effort from all concerned it has been just possible to make both ends meet.

By present-day standards the weekly subscription is ridiculously low, and we know it, but with the normal complement of thirteen members it does go a little way towards defraying expenses while remaining an individual outlay that everyone can afford.

### *COLLECTING*

In an inherently informal, somewhat haphazard, concern like this, it has not proved easy to devise a cast-iron scheme for collecting the weekly subscription. As the club is intended as far as possible to be self-run as well as self-sufficient, until recently the members took it in turns to do a four-week stint of this particular chore, but no plan seemed to be one-hundred-per-cent successful. No one would ever default by intent, but it is easy to forget, especially when the members are scattered around an area and do not always meet up every week.

Now the task has been taken over by an obliging father who charts in each payment, and the contributions are collected monthly instead of weekly. The contribution is suspended for absences of two weeks or more due to illness or holidays—which may not be good finance, but does make for good relations!

## *RAISING THE WIND*

With such a small subscription the bulk of the club income has to come from various enterprises organized by members and their families. Something that will bring in a reasonable sum in one go is preferable, but there are various smaller affairs that prove suprisingly profitable.

## *INDIVIDUAL EFFORTS*

An annual wine and cheese party, with a guest-speaker and innumerable friends packed into a small house, always produces an excellent result.

On a smaller scale, giving "pony rides" is another money-spinner. The "no riding by outsiders" rule is waived when the Twala Club is invited to bring a selection of ponies along to some suitable festivity. And as the organizers always seem to be sympathetic towards the club and consider the ponies' act as a "draw"—apart from a small contribution what is earned benefits our own finances. Pinocchio, Paint and Amber have the temperament best-suited to this kind of outing, and there is never any lack of member volunteers willing to take charge and present themselves and the ponies looking enticingly smart. In the interest of the ponies a time is fixed both for arrival and departure and no adults are catered for. In the interests of safety the ponies are led a specified distance, and no one is allowed to ride by themselves. In Jubilee Year, when the Twala Club was more in demand than usual, a very worthwhile sum was earned in this way, and each year "giving rides" produces a financial bonus.

## *HIRING THE PONIES*

When weekend riding only is possible during term-time, it seems reasonable that the ponies should be exercised, and at the same time earn something towards their keep, by being hired to suitable applicants.

The difficulty here is to ensure that applicants are "suitable" —genuine horsemen who are happy to take out mannered animals for a hack round the countryside in return for a reasonable contribution to funds, and the willingness to catch, saddle, bridle, and put away their mount, and rub up the tack afterwards.

It would be easy to advertise this facility to good financial effect in the local press, but much safer to do it only through the "grapevine". In this way the "hello-bellow" brigade, the types who consider they can ride if they can stay on a horse's back, are unlikely to be involved, and are certainly not required. But, providing they are of a size to ride ponies, there must be many retired people, or mothers of schoolchildren, who would like to renew the riding they once enjoyed It is a scheme which, once the insurance cover has been adjusted, the club hopes to get going to mutual advantage.

*FINES*

A small source of income even less popular with members than that derived from the collection of manure is that supplied by the fines they have to pay for leaving things—grooming-implements, head-collars, whips etc.,—scattered around, instead of in the tack room where they belong. The fine, 10p a head, is imposed on the entire membership regardless, which makes the system as unfair as it is unpopular, but does ensure that for some weeks at least transgressors are forcefully reminded by the guiltless to put their tackle away.

*COLLECTING PAPER*

In common with most of the Scout and Guide packs in the country, the Twala Club at one period industriously collected every type of waste paper to sell for re-pulping, and for a time this was quite a lucrative side-line. Unfortunately there was nowhere to keep it except in our garage and, when the scheme was overdone and the mills could take no more, for eighteen months we had to accept that most of the car's floor-space was given over to two tons of waste paper, plus attendant rodents. This is one source of revenue that is no longer encouraged.

## *THE CLUB DRAW*

With the aid of the smaller schemes, given the luck the club can then derive its income from three larger projects per year. In the past we have tried out hand at a Tramps' Supper and a Disco, but the most rewarding have proved to be an annual Lottery, a Barn Dance, at which the lottery prize-winners are drawn, and a Show.

No one needs to be told how to run a lottery, but experience has taught us the one or two points that ensure maximum profit. As with all our money-raisers, the draw is farmed out to one or another set of parents, and the organizers make quite sure that all the prizes—forty or so for six hundred books of tickets is a reasonable ratio—are value for money, with the first prize outstandingly attractive.

All the prizes are donated, so that apart from the cost of printing the tickets (an outlay that increases annually) the draw is clear profit. And although the tickets are five to a book, we try never to sell singles and find that few quibble at paying out 25p.

Selling tickets is not everyone's idea of fun, but all club members have to undertake to sell a given number, and to come back for more when those have been disposed of. And the fact that the continuance of the club depends on the success of these ventures spurs on the most diffident salesman.

## *BARN DANCE*

The club has only recently cashed in on the current vogue for a form of entertainment very suited to British horse-lovers, even if the connection is American.

The first essential is an authentic barn. The one we are loaned, situated in the appropriate venue of a lane called Donkey Street, is in farm use up to the day before the dance. The club then descends on it in force with an assortment of cobweb-brushes and, under the direction of an artistically-minded father, it is transformed with the aid of appropriate

15. *Paint takes a novice on her first effort at "bending" in a gymkhana.*

posters and a decorative selection of saddles and bridles along the beams.

A really good "group" with an experienced caller of the steps is the most important ingredient of a successful evening, with a committee capable of producing satisfactory eats at low cost coming a close second. Either a bar is provided, or people bring their own drink.

Fire insurance is one of many items that must never be forgotten, and admission "by ticket only" copes with the possible problem of "undesirables". To date the barn dances have proved sufficiently lucrative to make holding one worth while, and the evening has the added advantage of providing the type of get-together likely to be lacking in a club of this kind.

### *SHOW AND GYMKHANA*

Gone are the happy-go-lucky days when we provided a couple of "catchers" to field a minute rider who was apt to be jumped off by her microscopic pony each time she faced the

Chase-me-Charlie pole. No longer may a vociferous chorus of club members from the side-lines shout the way round the show-jumping course as they did in the days when Aunt Jabiska carried some fright-frozen rider on a first occasion of leaping in public. In common with other aspects of the club, our show format, and our attitude towards it, have had to be adapted to the demands of the years. And with each show the standard, and the profit target, have had to be raised.

Now we have reached our peak. The Twala Club Show remains unaffiliated, and is still noted for its friendly atmosphere, but with the loan of an exceptional site it is now possible to operate three rings, in addition to Clear Round jumping and a "fun" Exemption Dog Show. We now aspire to Open as well as Novice classes to bring in the maximum number of competitors. To tempt the adults further there is a Riding Horse Class, as well as two for different-sized Working Ponies. The Family Ponies are not forgotten—the youngest members have their own Minimus Jumping, and there are three different age-groups in the gymkhana games. A class that seems especially popular is an Open Horse-Pony Handy Horse Competition, comprising obstacle-course, gymkhana skills and jumping, all against the clock.

The Twala Club Show does not aspire to compare with all the hundreds of far larger, more rewarding and better organized affairs now put on all over the country. But given the one essential over which no one has any control—fine weather—it now attains its two main objectives: a happy day for those who support it, and a profit that makes all the hard work involved in running it well worth the effort.

### *GUIDE-LINES*

Everyone to their own show, but for what it is worth, experience has taught us a few "musts" for a day to be successful on all counts.

The date must be fixed early, preferably the previous year, to avoid clashing with too many other local shows. In our case the choice of date is limited to a time when none of our members is on holiday, and when the hay grown on the site of the show has been carried.

Advertising should start in good time, at least eight weeks before the date, with posters or schedules sent to local riding establishments, saddlers, corn merchants and branches of the Pony Club. The blacksmith will usually distribute schedules as he goes on his rounds. If possible, an advertisement or mention of the show should be got into the local press about two weeks before the actual day.

The show must finish in reasonable time, which is a difficult target to achieve but essential if the customers are to be kept happy right up to the end of the day, and a good attendance assured for the following year. It can be done if the following can be achieved:

—All officials arrive on the site at least an hour before the show is due to start, and they all know exactly how to do their own particular job, be it secretarial, collecting-ring steward or arena party. Needless to say everything, from rings and fences to "props" for the gymkhana, should have been made ready the day before. And in this era of vandalism we arrange for someone to sleep on the site, so that everything is as it should be when we arrive!
—In each ring the first class must start at the time advertised, even if the remainder of the times have to be approximate. And the number of entries in all Jumping classes must be limited, if the judges, and the show, are not to be overwhelmed.
—A commentator who is a good organizer and capable of holding things together and pushing it all along with humour, and military precision, is the final important cog in the timing wheel.

Other items to consider are:

—"Loos". Here we have discovered that the local Girl

Guides are often able to oblige with this essential, providing exactly what is needed for a most moderate charge.
—Judges and a course-builder who are experienced and well-known in the district help to bring in competitors, and their names should be included on the schedule. They give their service voluntarily, and are entitled to be given a reasonable lunch in return for a long and tiring day!

To ensure the maximum profit the club always endeavours, and so far with success, to get all the big expenses covered before the day of the show. Our prizes are normally money for the Jumping classes and the Riding Horse class, "in kind" for the

16. *The heraldic horse! Jason learns to show jump.*

remainder, and four rosettes for every class. Gymkhana winners are awarded rosettes only. It must be remembered that at an unaffiliated show where some of the classes are Open, and animals registered with either the B.S.J.A. or comparable showing society are entered, the first prize may not be more than £3. For this reason the entry fees are kept as low as is possible without forgoing reasonable profits.

"Win a rosette and out" is the rule for our Clear Round jumping, and with the ponies in mind each competitor is limited to four tries. We like to finish the day with Barrel Elimination, or a Ribbon Race—run in pairs against the clock. There is an annual running-battle over including a Chase-me-Charlie, a competition devised to my mind to over-face the entries, but beloved of all contestants!

### *RUMMAGE AND RIDE*

This money-spinner jumble sale is a Twala Club special that has the merits of being relatively easy and quick to organize, and appealing, for no apparent reason, to a number of people. It cannot always be fitted in amongst the other enterprises, but is a standby when funds are at a dangerously low ebb. And now that we have our "complex" of shelters the affair is no longer so dependent on good weather.

Its preparation consists merely of keeping the ponies out of the shelters for a week or so in advance, and then putting down a thick layer of clean straw. The date has therefore to be fixed before the carrying of the hay crop. The rummage is laid out on a "table" of wooden pallets running the length of the hay store. A junk-stall is set up in one shelter, two or three games of chance of the Tombola variety in the other. Members give pony-rides in the schooling field across the lane, and at some stage put on a musical ride, if time allows for learning it, or a display of jumping.

The entire affair is put together in the morning and takes place in the afternoon of the same day, and people do come, and do spend—and club funds benefit surprisingly.

## Chapter Seven

# MONEY MATTERS—SPENDING IT

Having boosted the Twala Club "kitty" by our various money-making enterprises, we are unpleasantly surprised each year at the speed with which it empties again. But then ponies, even ponies kept collectively and living out as economically as possible, are expensive creatures—and some more so than others.

Feeding is of course the most costly item, and since it also comprises the most important aspect of good pony-keeping the subject has a chapter to itself. Otherwise the money goes on field and general maintenance, and other inescapable and recurring expenses, plus a host of smaller items that seem of little monetary moment until they are all added up.

### *SHOEING*

"No foot, no horse" is one of the most hackneyed clichés in the horse world, but none the less true for that. Like Fiddler, some ponies have good, hard feet. They may well need a "remove" and their hooves trimmed, the odd clench knocked back, in between shoeing sessions, but otherwise their shoes normally stay put until worn out. Feet like this present few if any problems, need comparatively little spent on them and, unlike Jason's, are a joy to owner and blacksmith alike.

### *DIFFICULT FEET*

Jason, whose hooves are light-coloured, and originally soft and shelly, had been running out without shoes for a couple of years when we took him on, and his feet were so worn it was problematical whether he could be shod at all. For the first few months a lot of time was spent in searching fields for shoes the cob had shed, so that at least the same ones could be replaced. The farrier almost took up residence and, apart from the cost, the constant nailing on was scarcely the treatment required. On the other hand Jason was better shod than not, and very gradually his feet improved sufficiently to hold a set of shoes for a reasonable time. Now his feet still need constant watching as they are liable to crack and break away, but daily dressing with "sump" oil, applied below the coronet, plus an occasional course of cod-liver oil taken internally—the equivalent of two tablespoonsful spread over a week and given in his food—have greatly improved matters. This cob will never have very good feet, but at least they are now passable and it is possible to keep him adequately shod.

Care of the feet is not something that can ever be neglected, but although the ponies do a proportion of road work it is not sufficient to wear their shoes out quickly. Risen clenches are dealt with as necessary, and according to the time of year—hoof grows more slowly in winter—removes and trimming may be needed every four or five weeks, but the ponies are not newly shod more than is strictly requisite.

### *NO SHOES*

Some of the ponies are not shod at all. After his first year with us, at the farrier's suggestion Spotty always went barefoot, without harm. Amber has not been shod for years and has feet of iron, and Pinocchio's have improved since his shoes were dispensed with. But this idea has to be tried out with the greatest caution and, it must be emphasized, even where no road work at all is involved it is possible to work only some ponies without shoes—usually those that are native-bred and therefore nearer to the wild. The policy could well be disastrous with anything approaching a Thoroughbred, or an animal with weak or shelly feet. Any pony with which it is tried must have a more or less true action, so that the hoof is worn down evenly on both front and both hind feet. We had no success with Paint because he "dishes", and the uneven wear on his off-fore soon reduced him to being footsore—a condition easy to recognize even in the early stages. Once on the road the pony makes a bee-line for the verge and does its best to remain there.

When Spot was shoeless his feet seldom needed trimming, but occasionally required to be levelled. Amber's dark-coloured, Exmoor hooves have to be cut back quite frequently. They are so hard that work does not wear them down, and so tough that the farrier has difficulty in getting his knife through the horn. On arrival Pinocchio's feet looked boxy and rather donkey-like, with slightly contracted heels. Since allowing him to go shoeless his heels have opened up and the frogs, in contact with the ground as they should be, have become really prominent. Even his owner agrees that this pony appears happier and goes better without shoes. It seems probable that Fiddler would be a good candidate for the same idea, and in the coming winter when the ground is soft the theory may be put to the test.

### *THE FARRIER*

Nowadays shoeing-smiths are comparatively rare birds; the majority have more work than they know what to do with, and of necessity their prices have risen sharply, some more than others. The experts in this field are worth their weight in gold, but unfortunately are so sought after that with the best will in the world they can not always come just when needed. And sometimes it is a question either of having a pony that has lost a shoe out of work for a couple of weeks while it awaits the attention of the first-class man, or of making do with a farrier who is adequate, if less of a craftsman, but is able to come within days. The "cowboy" farriers, cashing in on a general need but without proper training, should be avoided like the devil!

Regardless of the season of the year, our long-suffering blacksmith often shoes the club ponies out in the open, because of the normally muddy entrance to our sheds and the poor light inside. And there are not so many of his exacting trade who would undertake to do that.

## *VETERINARY OUTLAY*

If ponies are to be properly cared for there are some veterinary charges that are unavoidable, and that come round as regularly as the call of the cuckoo.

## *WORMING*

All horses and ponies of whatever size or shape have to be wormed regularly if they are to thrive. If they live out, and particularly where the fields are small, this aspect of good horsemastership is even more important and the animals must be wormed that much more frequently.

Until recently none of the effective wormers was particularly palatable, and although a minority of horses and ponies will eat just about anything, the majority tended to take one sniff and go on strike. Our worst time with this difficulty was in the spring of 1977. After the previous glorious hot summer the larvae of the bot-flies, which normally complete part of their life-cycle inside a horse with little or no ill effect, were so numerous in the locality that they were causing trouble. Our vet advised treatment that would put paid to them as well as to the more normal complement of worms.

It struck me that any horse would be a fool to have anything to do with the sky-blue granules supplied, even when, after being left standing for the prescribed time, the dose ceased to give off noxious fumes and was mixed in with a tasty meal of oats, bran and sugar.

Surprisingly, Spotty decided the whole thing was delicious and golluped it all down within minutes. It took the best part of a day to get even a proportion of the physic inside the other five ponies. Fiddler, commonly the slowest eater, fiddled his portion round and round and round the bucket, only swallowing such morsels as I managed to stuff between his teeth because he has an obliging nature. Three of the others were not much better, and had the grains not been too costly to waste, after two hours spent on Paint I would have abandoned him to his bots without a qualm.

### *PRESENT METHODS*

After that episode, even though the ponies were not quite as reluctant to eat the more usual type of wormer, it seemed value for money to use the small plungers which, when inserted in the corner of the mouth, discharge a sticky paste that cannot be rejected. These, however, had to be abandoned when the price went even higher, and we now use a slightly less costly but most effective powder, that is readily eaten even by the most suspicious when mixed in with the feed.

All the ponies are wormed every four to five months, but given two doses with a week's interval between—a method considered more effective than a single dose every six to eight weeks. Looked at over the year it is not a cheap exercise in pony-care, but it is an essential one.

### *ANTI-TETANUS*

Nearly all our loaned ponies have been immunized before they come to us, and, like the others, only need the annual booster until re-immunization becomes necessary. If they have not been done before, they are fully immunized as quickly as possible. It is money well-spent to counter a terrible risk no one should be prepared to take.

### *ANTI-FLU INJECTIONS*

Because there are many different viruses some people have as little faith in vaccination against equine influenza as against the human variety. But our family have vivid recollections of the year when all the time, food, and excitement expended on Twala to get him fit for his first inclusion in the local team for the Pony Eventing Championship was brought to nothing by an attack of flu three days before the competition.

Admittedly Twala Club ponies do not mix with others as frequently as most of the competing fraternity, and therefore run less risk of infection, but, apart from any harmful effects of the illness, it seems worth trying to ensure that they are all well and workable for the summer holidays when they are most in demand.

*THE UNEXPECTED*

Apart from occasional teeth-rasping, which although not a regular event comes into the category of normal veterinary care, the essentials listed above account for the "unavoidable" medical expenditure. But although to date we have been very lucky with the ponies, provision has to be made for the sudden illnesses and accidents that appear out of the blue.

*TENDON TROUBLE*

Jabiska and her feet were a case in point, and an expensive one at that. Then there was the year Amber decided to play rough galloping games with Jason on an area of field that had been badly poached and then baked hard by the sun. We found him dead lame, unable in fact to put his grossly swollen near-fore to the ground. This was a case of a sprained tendon, one of the classic injuries suffered by racehorses and others where speed is a major requirement. The vet applied a special bandage that stayed put, and Amber was sound in six weeks. Two months later he did the same thing, this time playing with Fiddler. Once more the same treatment proved equally effective, and he has remained sound since.

*REFLEX CONTRACTION OF THE DIAPHRAGM*

I greeted the curious information a breathless member had rushed to tell me with sceptical calmness. "Paint," she panted, "has hiccups! Is it all right to ride him?" I had never heard of a horse having hiccups, and did not believe they could, but, as always, the matter had to be investigated.

Paint was hitched to the rail in the schooling field. He looked his usual unruffled self, but as we watched he burped unmistakably, and then burped again. There was no doubt about it. Here was a pony with hiccups. But whether it mattered, or if it might be the symptoms of some dire disease, was beyond me. He continued to burp as I came up to him, inadvertently on the windward side, only to have another shock. Paint was also suffering from bad breath . . . very bad breath. Another cautious sniff and the odour was unmistakable—onions!

Our vet is used to being rung up and faced with occasionally bizarre Twala Club queries, but this one momentarily floored him. He had never heard of a horse eating onions, let alone being affected by them—but then not many of his clients would be inhabiting fields where the wild variety grows. After a pause for thought he came to the conclusion that so long as Paint ceased hiccuping in a reasonable time there seemed little cause for worry. And, in fact, an hour's quiet hack effected a cure. But the ponies are now kept out of that field when the grass is scant and the onion crop in evidence.

### *OEDEMA*

Paint seems to go in for out-of-the-way ailments. Another agitated rider came running to report that while out on a ride she had noticed a swelling on the pony's neck, and by the time they got home it was so large he could scarcely turn his head. Sure enough there was a lump, by then the size of a small melon, on Paint's neck about a hand's breadth from his gullet. It seemed to be painless, and again the patient was unperturbed. By the time the vet came the lump was slightly smaller, and as it was sited on the neck muscle and still painless he decided the best treatment was to "wait and see". There was a tiny "pit" on top of the swelling and the only feasible suggestion was that it was caused by a sting, possibly a hornet. The lump gradually subsided and there were no ill effects, but the episode had a sequel. A few months later it was embarrassing to have called the vet out to examine another swelling in Paint's neck, this time underneath in the region of his gullet—only to be informed that this pony's thyroid gland was, naturally, slightly more prominent than most!

### *UNSUSPECTED MALAISE*

Next to Jabiska, Fiddler provided our worst and most

expensive medical problem. But although my failure to realize how "out of sorts" he was feeling was inexcusable, fortunately Fiddler's case has had a happy ending.

The pony was not "right" for a long while before it was realized he was suffering from mild but chronic azoturia. The condition was accentuated in the summer when he started Pony Club eventing and was entered in a tetrathlon, and although not stabled, was being "fed up" (and exercised) in a bid to get him as fit as possible. At that time he looked well, but his performance gradually worsened, and his outlook became more and more lackadaisical. Eventually, when he packed up at the first fence across-country, it at last dawned that his uncharacteristic behaviour had nothing to do with over-facing or sourness or incorrect riding. The vet was called in and the condition diagnosed.

By this time the summer was over. Fiddler's diet was restricted to such grass as remained, unlimited hay, and grass-nuts. He was better, but scarcely "sparkled" even when hunting. On the other hand he is by nature quiet and inclined to indolence, and it was assumed he could never be "hotted up"—without the concentrates we dare not give him for fear of exacerbating the azoturia condition. He continued to jump adequately indoors, but seemed to tire easily and then once more began refusing across-country. A bad, and totally uncharacteristic, attack of apparent claustrophobia when travelling confirmed our suspicions that still all was far from well with him.

A blood test endorsed our doubts. As laymen we gathered that although Fiddler's blood-count was not drastically wrong, it was sufficiently so to form a kind of vicious circle with the azoturia, each condition affecting the other. And although his red-worm count was not high by normal standards, as red-worms are so called because they feed on blood, they too were contributing to the general malaise.

Treatment began at once with an injection of steroids, followed by a course of follic acid, and worming every seventh day for three weeks. A dose of a concentrated preparation containing all the vitamins, trace elements, riboflavin etc. that any horse in his condition could need, was mixed in with his daily feed of grass-nuts for a couple of months.

"In six weeks you won't know him!" the vet assured us.

Within a month Fiddler was a different pony. By the end of the prescribed time he looked an eyeful, was full of energy and "sauce" and pulling into his fences with all his original verve and enjoyment. He was so full of himself that he was thinking it funny not to be caught, and from the meek animal that gave way to all the other ponies, had changed into the herd boss of all but Paint.

Fiddler is the living example of how stupid and unfair it can be to the animal concerned not to investigate thoroughly a horse's physical condition before assuming that any change in normal behaviour, however slight, is due to laziness, "sourness", or something of the kind.

*ACCIDENTS*

To date, apart from the inevitable allotment of slight cuts and injuries that respond to home treatment, the club ponies have suffered no other serious illnesses; but there is always the risk of an accident.

Jason managed to break down part of a fence and got a length of barbed wire in the groove at the back of his pastern. The resulting cut was deep and extensive and required the attention of the vet, but with the aid of a prescribed antibiotic cream applied twice daily, it healed surprisingly quickly.

Pinocchio had the misfortune to tread on the base of a broken bottle that was hidden in long grass. It was too firmly imbedded in his hind hoof for his rider to move him and the vet had to be summoned to the site of the accident. Fortunately this was not very far from the pony's field, and after removal of the glass the foot was bandaged and he was led home. An immediate injection of antibiotics had to be followed by one on each of the succeeding three days, administered by ourselves.

17. *Fiddler demonstrates that home-made fences produce a versatile jumper.*

And I discovered that throwing a needle into a horse's neck, as done by a veterinary surgeon, is not as easy as it looks. However, the treatment, supplemented by poultices on the foot followed by a "blue" spray of gentian, brought speedy recovery from what could have been a more serious accident.

### *MEDICINE CHEST*

Our medical supplies are not extensive, but money has to be expended to keep up a stock of essential first-aid remedies. These include cotton wool, "Animaltex" for poulticing, and bandages or broad adhesive plaster for holding it in place, embrocation and a tin of kaolin paste. The remedy most frequently in use is a "puffer" of antibiotic wound powder.

If not exactly medicinal, fly-spray and shampoo are both used regularly throughout the summer and neither are cheap commodities. They are now bought in bulk, and doled out as required into "squeezy" plastic containers that previously contained washing-up liquid.

### *TACK MAINTENANCE*

The annual expenditure on saddle-soap and leather-oil is a pointer to the fact that, however unpopular in principle with some members, regular tack cleaning is carried out. Safety, as well as good maintenance of the excellent tack loaned with the ponies, demands that all repairs are attended to promptly, replacements made as necessary, and saddles re-stuffed when they require it. We are lucky to have the service of a saddler who is efficient, quick, and reasonable in his charges.

### *RUGS*

The club has acquired an assortment of rugs, only used between classes, at shows or when travelling, one of them a smart checked summer sheet, dating back to 1890 when it was worn by a driving pony belonging to a great-aunt. Our type of pony does not normally require a New Zealand rug when living out, particularly now that there is adequate shelter in all the fields, but, like Jabiska, Jason grows so fine a winter coat that he needs additional protection.

The cob brought his own rug with him, but his addiction to leaning on barbed wire soon put paid to that. It was renovated at considerable expense while he took on, and quickly demolished, an ancient affair that had been Jabiska's. When the mended rug went the same way, a new one was bought at an outlay club finances could have done without—that, with the addition of a patch or two, still survives, but for how long is problematical. Short of enclosing Jason in armour, or investing in post and rail fencing, the problem seems insoluble. It is not only on account of the grazing that the Twala Club looks for the warm days of spring!

Taffy was clipped when he arrived, but had been furnished with a brand-new New Zealand rug by his thoughtful owner, out to resolve any stabling dilemmas. A bleak, cold spring meant he wore his rug much longer than intended, but it is still in one piece. The pony will obviously not be clipped in future, but it is a boon to have a spare rug of this kind to use in case of illness.

### *PROTECTIVE APPAREL*

Since losing his excessive fat and becoming better balanced through schooling, Jason no longer requires the same amount of shielding from self-damage—the "gaiters", over-reach boots, etc., that were formerly essential. It is still safer to put on what are known as his "wellies" for any form of competitive jumping, and it is just our bad luck that the number he manages to split have to be the largest, and therefore the most expensive, size!

Apart from these necessities the ponies all wear leg-bandages over gamgee, and tail-bandages, when travelling. And since Fiddler's bout of claustrophobia, he is more or less encased in sheets of cotton-wool, gamgee, foam rubber and anything else suitable to hand, in case the trouble should recur.

### *INSURANCE*

This subject has been touched on in the chapter on acquiring ponies, but in addition to paying all or part of the premiums on animals under ten years old, and on part of the most valuable tack, the other saddles and bridles are covered by an all-in policy that includes theft and fire. From the beginning the club has held an essential public liability policy, covering damage by ponies and/or riders. Each year, once the hay is carried and in store, that too is ensured against fire and theft.

Now that some of the ponies hunt occasionally, this risk is covered by payment of a small additional sum. The chief problem with insurance is that, like everything else, the premiums are frequently raised.

### *ENTRY FEES*

When the club first embarked on eventing the chosen shows were the small affairs best suited to our, very novice, standard. There were not many, and in those halcyon days the entry fees were delightfully low and the club could cope with paying most or all of them. Sometimes a small money-making project was got up to provide a special fund for the purpose.

Nowadays the general running costs of the club preclude keeping funds for any special purposes, and all entry fees have risen to the point where competing at any type of show means quite an outlay on the day. In our case, as our standards and ambition rise, the type of show we try to attend is on a slightly higher level too, and the entry fees comparable. It is now impossible for club funds to provide for everyone or even make part payments each time, but when the state of the bank balance allows the club contributes towards what can be a distinct problem for parents.

### *TRAVELLING EXPENSES*

In the early days there were only two or three suitable shows a season that were beyond the range of the ponies' four legs. When we did travel it was possible to afford doing so in style, hiring an enormous box for a very moderate charge. The then four club ponies were packed in, leaving room for at least a couple of "friends" whose owners shared the expenses, and it was all fun, vastly convenient, and a treat for everyone including our friend the driver. Now, the costs of running such a vehicle, combined with overtime rates, have brought the hiring charges to a point that would swallow up the Twala Club's entire travelling allowance for the season in one day's outing, and we are more than lucky on occasions to have an alternative.

The club still gets to as many shows as possible on its own feet, sometimes putting up for the night en route. For longer distances one of the club's most generous and helpful friends sometimes loans us a landrover and big trailer that takes two of the larger ponies and one smaller one. The long-suffering club father who drives it is a wizard on maintenance, and the good care he takes of the combination is set off against wear and tear so that our only expense is the fuel.

Club competing at "away" shows is still on a very moderate scale, and even when the trailer is available normally riders and ponies have to take it in turns to go. But sometimes, if the distance is not too great, our once unhorse-minded driver, now rapidly becoming a horse addict, is prepared to make two trips, which adds up to a considerable mileage. It does mean, however, that the club can occasionally compete in full force.

Competing beyond our immediate area is limited also by the state of the club exchequer, and that of the parents concerned, as well as by the number of Saturdays or Sundays (when we can borrow the trailer) it seems fair to involve our indispensable driver. But one way and another we contrive to have a lot of fun, if not quite as much as some riders would wish.

### *FENCING*

It may seem odd that the annual fencing bills should be high. Once a fence is adequately erected, except for occasional running repairs that should seem to be the end of the matter until the posts actually start rotting. But owing to the club's peculiar grazing arrangements, or lack of them, some fencing project or other nearly always seems to be in hand—either enclosing a new plot, or de-fencing one from which we have been asked to remove ourselves. And although in the latter case, in the interests of economy, our posts and wire go with us, the new field is usually larger or different-shaped and requires more materials. As for the "move", anyone who has experienced rolling up used barbed wire will understand why this chore is one of those least enjoyed by the parents who undertake it.

In these days posts, barbed wire, even the staples that hold them together, add up to quite a considerable outlay over the year. And more are usually required for existing fences during the winter, when grass is scarce, the odd blade over the fence irresistibly tempting, and barriers need to be strengthened or heightened. Experience has taught us that a single-strand guard rail, placed three or four feet out from a fence, is nearly impossible to breach.

Originally most of our "gates" were elderly sheep-hurdles, acquired from neighbouring farms and brought up to the required height with a strand of barbed wire along the top. Spot put paid to one or two of these, and the others collapsed from old age. Nowadays we have to invest in much larger, tougher and more costly cattle-wattles, but even these do not always stand up to the attentions of Taffy and Pinocchio, both "bangers of gates" when food is in the vicinity—Taffy inflicting the most damage, more quickly, because he is shod.

Whatever the reasons, fencing does make an annual hole in the club budgeting, but the work entailed has another more commendable side-effect: several club fathers, normally employed in sedentary occupations, are developing biceps that would do credit to a Mr. World!

## *Chapter Eight*

# FEEDING

If you keep ponies you have to feed them adequately but with sense. They must always have sufficient food for the work that is required of them—that is, sufficient to keep them looking and feeling right summer and winter alike, but over-stuffing a pony with oats is no more correct feeding than keeping it on short rations would be. The type of pony, the amount of work, the capabilities of the rider, all have to be taken into account and each animal then fed as an individual. And as the years have taught us, keeping ponies collectively provides excellent opportunities for finding out some of the answers by trial and error.

### *THE CHANGING SCENE*

When the club began it did not occur to me that our requirements in the type of pony needed might change with the years, with the consequence that our feed bills would increase by leaps and bounds. The club's annually increasing expenditure on food is not entirely due to inflation.

Certainly in those early days the price of everything from hay to cubes had not started rocketing towards its present height, but our feed bills were relatively low anyway because of the modest ability of our riders, and any idea of serious competing remained a pipe-dream of the future. At that time, in theory, club requirements meant that the ponies could thrive on a diet composed principally of grass in summer and unlimited hay in winter.

## *INDIVIDUAL NEEDS*

As often happens, in practice the theory did not always work out. A late spring, an unusually hard winter or over-dry summer, anything on those lines could upset the apple-cart, not to mention the different needs of different animals, which in those days mainly meant Aunt Jabiska.

Twala, a "good doer" by any standards, presented no problems and would have been beyond his riders' abilities if fed as he used to be. Spotty, even by the time his riders had his measure and he was beginning to cover himself with glory at gymkhanas, had always to be fed concentrates with the greatest caution. Like most small ponies, with the exception of the Ambers of this world, give Spot little more than a token amount of "hard feed" and he could get distinctly above himself. But Jabiska's large, gaunt frame, even when in the lightest work, needed more than hay and grass to keep it reasonably covered. No one would ever dispute that by temperament she was worth her weight in gold, but in other ways that old grey mare was a living demonstration of the fact that buying a flat-sided, slack-loined case of malnutrition is usually poor economy!

18. *A good day for Pinocchio, his clear round earns a reward.*

## *THE ART OF FEEDING*

As any old-time groom will tell you, feeding is an art and, whatever the branch of competitive riding, much of the success of the top-notchers lies in their ability to combine correct feeding with correct exercise and so keep their horse at the required peak of fitness. But it is an art that cannot be taught by rule of thumb. The general principles can be assimilated—after that it is a case of common and horse sense, observation, and trial and error. And one of the first rules with ponies is to assess their type. A blood animal might well not thrive on the amount of concentrates that would keep a hard-working native-bred pony in tiptop condition. Conversely, give that kind of animal the quantities necessary for a highly-bred pony in full work, and it can become ill or unmanageable.

An associate member of the Twala Club, a good little rider and real horse-lover, eventually achieved her dream of having her own pony. It was a young New Forest gelding, bought from someone who had "rescued" it as a case of debility, and after a few months, although much improved in condition, it was still on the thin side.

The family are all devoted to the pony, and its welfare takes a first place in their lives, but they have no background of horse. Quite correctly, as the pony was a four-year-old, he was brought along slowly despite outstanding jumping ability, but that first winter was a hard one and he ceased to put on flesh and did not appear to be thriving as he should. An expert summoned several times for advice suggested this and that, including the feeding of large quantities of concentrates, and the pony began to pick up and look really well. What the expert did not realize, and no one took into consideration, was that through those weeks of dark winter evenings in term-time, the pony could only be ridden at weekends.

Always a gay ride, he soon began playing up, on the road as well as anywhere else, using the sight of any traffic as an excuse for bucking and taking off until his rider was almost afraid to take him out. The family, worried but pleased with the handsome eyeful their pony had become, continued conscientiously to follow the advice on feeding—until it was suggested that it was not much good having a pony that looked and obviously was in splendid condition, if it was also unrideable!

The concentrates were then cut down relating to the amount of exercise involved, to a quantity that the pony could assimilate without getting "above himself". As the spring grass came, if not in quite such hard condition he acquired nicely rounded contours in all the right places—and in behaviour returned to what he was by temperament, a super animal that is fun to ride anywhere.

Of the present club ponies, when they are in regular work and competing, Pinocchio's performance and outlook are improved by a ration of the "hard stuff", and Amber can take quite a lot for a pony of his size without its going to his head. Jason remains his usual exuberant self regardless of how he is fed, but in winter, or when competing, needs concentrates daily to keep him in good condition. Taffy is another who is inexhaustible even off grass, but takes a lot out of himself and is given hard feed as necessary.

By temperament Fiddler could well do with concentrates when he is competing, but although the vet thinks he will outgrow his propensity to azoturia he cannot yet take them in any form without showing signs of stiffening up. In summer he therefore competes, perforce, off grass, and so long as he is exercised regularly and does not get too fat, does so with much success. In winter he receives grass-nuts in addition to unlimited hay.

Now that summer eventing at Pony Club level has been added to the Twala Club's programme, with the exception of Fiddler all the ponies' rations have been stepped up and their intake of grass limited to a degree, with a consequent rise in costs. And one advantage of some of the curious little fields in our possession is that we do not have the bother of shutting the ponies in to control their figures, during the influx of spring and early summer grass. Any animal that shows signs of becoming too gross is switched to one of these scanty plots that are guaranteed to keep a pony's bulk within bounds.

The chief drawback to such grazing is that red-worms lay their eggs on the lower end of grass stalks, and close cropping can mean re-infection.

### *HAY*

Hay provides nutrition—more, or less, according to quality—and also the bulk and fibrous roughage essential to a horse's digestive processes when grass is lacking. On the type of rough pasture that the club ponies graze, their winter hay needs work out approximately at a minimum of one ton per head—and if all our hay had to be bought at current prices we should certainly not be able to afford six animals. As it is we make as much of our own as we can, including that taken from the two acres some miles away. Some seasons provide almost sufficient for our needs, in others a couple of tons may have to be bought, but whatever the source the club has learned the truth of the axiom that "poor hay is poor economy". In the hot summer of '76 our hay crop could be smelled, wafted sweet as honey on the breeze, long before reaching the hay store. After cutting there had not been a drop of rain to spoil it, and it had been possible to carry it the day after cutting so that none of the nutritional value was lost, but owing to drought there was not much of it. The quality was so good, however, that the ponies did not waste so much as a wisp, and thrived on about two-thirds of the daily ration necessary a year later. That was the season when for the first time, owing to a liberal application of fertilizer, our hay field grew a really abundant crop of grass, but only a few hours after it was cut the weather turned sour. During the next ten days we struggled at prescribed intervals to turn these tons of soggy grass as the top layer dried sufficiently, and each time the rain plummeted down to make it wasted effort. The crop was taken in the end, mainly because it would have meant complete disaster if it was not, but there was a high percentage of waste. Of what remained, and it was fortunate that there was still a great deal, the bulk of the "goodness" had been lost, together with all the "nose". The ponies did eat it and it provided the necessary bulk, but they squandered so much in their efforts to pick out the best that in addition to several pounds of concentrates we ended up feeding each of them a 16 lb net of hay at night, and a further 8 or 9 lbs in the morning. Under normal conditions the ponies are fed as much hay as they will clear up, averaging about 11-12 lbs each per day.

### *STRAW*

At a pinch, a proportion (up to 50 percent) of clean barley or oat straw can be mixed with the hay ration and fed to ponies on very light work. The Club has access to barley straw from our farm, but the ponies make it plain that they prefer straight hay. Oat straw is more palatable than barley, but is almost unobtainable in this district.

### *MAKING HAY*

At one time a local farmer used to cut and bale our hay, and to save expense the members and parents turned it in the old-fashioned way with hand-rakes. But as hay-making always comes in term-time and seldom at weekends, this hard work always fell to the lot of the same too few stalwarts. Nowadays all the actual hay-making is undertaken by a contractor, and then carried with the aid of a borrowed tractor and trailer and the club's communal efforts over a few hours.

With finances as limited as those of the Twala Club even the costs of having the hay made seem considerable, but are nothing compared with what the outlay would be if it all had to be bought. Until recently it was a nightmare having to vacate our largest field by at least mid-March in order to grow the crop, when each year brought up the question of where on earth to accommodate the ponies at a time when grass is at a premium. One might have gambled on the season producing so lavish a hay crop that the price dropped to acceptable levels, but the risk was not worth taking. And now that the grazing acreage has been enlarged, it is not one that has to be contemplated.

## *FEEDING HAY*

The ponies are fed the bulk of their hay ration in nets in the evening. It is done by club members aided by their parents, and worked on a weekly rota system that gives each lot of "feeders" about three turns in the season. In term-time the feeding is done perforce after school, and for much of the winter that means in the dark. Mostly it is the mothers who get landed with helping their young because their husbands are still at work, and this is one of the chores that brings home to the previously unhorse-minded just what hard work is involved in pony-keeping.

The nets, collected by myself each morning, are filled in the hay shed in the evening by the light of a torch and weighed on a small spring balance as required. (The amount of hay varies a little according to weather conditions and the requirements of different ponies in different fields.) There are usually at least a couple of ponies milling around outside the store, eager

19. *The mothers help with the evening hay rota.*

for their ration and quick to snatch at the nearest net as the feeders emerge, and this is when occasional mishaps occur. If the ground round the sheds is in its usual winter state of being poached ankle-deep it is difficult enough to keep one's balance when humping a heavy net, without receiving a violent tug from behind. More than one parent new to the club, and more than innocent of the ways of ponies, has returned home from feeding plastered in mud from head to foot! Yet they never complain, and within days even the most apprehensive mother can be seen enforcing discipline and treating the ponies with a familiarity she would have deemed impossible before.

Any supplementary morning feeding of hay, normally only necessary during periods of frost and snow, is done by myself in term-time, as it would be unrealistic to expect members to cope with this chore before getting off to school. Regrettably, lack of time compels me to give this feed of hay by the least economical method—that is dumping "biscuits", shaken out in the required number of separate heaps in each field, either in the open or in corners in the shelters according to wind and weather. Ponies being what they are, this system entails considerable waste, but stopping to fill nets is an impossibility—and even the most long-suffering parent might go on strike if asked to fill double the quantity of nets at the evening stint. The problem might be solved by acquiring some wooden hay-racks, of the type formerly used for cattle, but they are not easy to come by.

Whatever the method employed, and whether the feed is of hay or concentrates, the feeders ensure that each net or pile or bowl is well away from the next. There is always a boss amongst horses or ponies, and one or other will do his best to get the lion's share.

### *SOAKING HAY*

Like many ponies, Paint is allergic to hay or hay dust and develops a cough and breathing akin to being broken-winded unless his hay is soaked prior to feeding. When we first had him the merest wisp of dry hay was sufficient to set him off. Now he can cope with small amounts, but his large evening net has to be thoroughly "dunked". Many people consider that all horses are better for having their hay treated in this way, and if time and labour allowed this would be done for all the club ponies. As it is, during winter Paint is either kept by himself or with one companion who also then receives soaked hay.

### *CONCENTRATES*

All horse food, including the bulk foods of young grass and good hay, contain some of the fats, starches (converted to sugar by the gastric juices) and protein that, together with water and fibrous roughage, are essential to equine health *when combined with the correct amount of exercise.* But "concentrates" is the collective name usually given to the specialized energy-producing foods necessary for horses and ponies doing more than light work. If the proportion of these foods is incorrect for the animal's energy output, then horse or pony will either lose condition and strength, in extreme cases to the point where it can die, or if receiving too much for the amount of exercise entailed, will become too fat. And surplus weight may mean digestive upsets, including in some cases azoturia, colic, laminitis, and physical strains.

Put at its simplest, the concentrates consist principally of differing ratios of the carbohydrates that produce heat and energy, and the proteins that are mainly responsible for the sustenance and growth of body tissue, replacement of muscular wastage, plus some supply of energy. The protein factor is more difficult to digest if there is too large a proportion of carbohydrate. Without protein, the carbohydrates cannot produce the energy that is their main function.

However much care and thought is given to the matter, a pony's exact requirements in the feeding of concentrates is not easy to assess, and can only be based on the reactions of the individual under different conditions of work. There are those who work their animals too hard on too little food; equally there is a school of thought that considers that many native-bred ponies—animals that still possess their native, very efficient and economical digestive system—are pampered, being given far less work than is good for them and fed an amount of "hard tack" they do not need and are better without.

We do our best, and sometimes that is right and sometimes wrong, but one lesson we have learned is that different forms of concentrates suit different ponies. This is something to bear in mind, even though in our case their feeding is largely based on what is available.

### *OATS*

This grain, lightly crushed, bruised or occasionally fed whole, and mixed with a small proportion of bran and a larger one of chaff, is the traditional ration for horses. It is considered the best and most digestible energy-producer, and is especially suitable for high-class animals in full work. But oats can be dangerously heady stuff for small ponies, and Spotty, Amber and Briggy never receive so much as a sniff of them. Nowadays they are also expensive; good broad bran is hard to get and no longer cheap, and few people now possess a chaff-cutter. (Chaff, which is a mixture of chopped hay and oat straw, can be bought "ready made", but there is no guarantee that it has been produced from good-class materials.)

Without doubt Thoroughbreds and horses competing in the top echelons thrive on oats, but there are other foods often more suited to the majority of our type of pony. Jason sometimes gets a ration, but it was this grain, stupidly fed in excess to Fiddler in an effort to get him fit for eventing, that precipitated his bout of azoturia. (Although, in fairness it should be said that the same quantities of any concentrate would probably have had the same effect.)

### *BARLEY*

This grain is less "intoxicating" than oats, and in some parts of the world constitutes much of the horses' rations. In the

Middle East it is often fed whole, which could explain why colic is such a common complaint there.

In winter, with the exception of Fiddler, all the Twala Club ponies receive a proportion of boiled barley, with a handful of soaked and well simmered linseed added in hard weather. This is no feed for extensive hard work, but it is a good filler for ponies living out, does not have the hotting-up properties of oats, helps to keep the flesh on them, and in our case is a money-saver, because we grow barley on our own farm.

### *MAIZE*

"Corn" is the staple diet of American horses and, despite the price, flaked maize is becoming increasingly popular in this country. It is good feed, but low in protein and, fed in excess of energy output, is very fattening. Jason's originally vast dimensions were partly due to the relished half-bucket of flaked maize he had been receiving daily. The club ponies get a proportion of flaked maize when funds run to feeding them an excellent "mixture" concocted by a local saddler.

### *BRAN*

Even if it is not used regularly for food, it is always handy to have some bran in store. Worm-powders and other physic mix in well with a little damp bran, the traditional bran mash is easily digested, indispensable in some cases of illness, and a much appreciated treat after hunting.

Bran has little actual food value and is too rich in phosphorous to be used too liberally, but is a good filler. Dry bran, fed on its own, is liable to choke the pony. This is very alarming for both pony and owner and a hazard to be avoided, but, as our vet assured me when it happened to Fiddler, in ninety-nine cases out of a hundred the flow of saliva effectively solves the problem in an hour or so.

### *BEANS*

Like linseed cake, beans are very nutritious, but as they are also very heating must be fed with caution and in small quantities. A handful, previously bruised or split, can be a useful adjunct to a concentrate feed for ponies living out in winter, but it must be stressed that some ponies "hot up" to the point of becoming unmanageable.

*CUBES*

Pelleted food for horses is a relatively modern innovation, now very popular if no longer cheap. Cubes are palatable, a controlled source of proteins and carbohydrates, clean and simple to use. They all contain added vitamins and minerals, but the concentrates are in different proportions according to brand and purpose. The bulk of our ponies' hard food comes in this form, either a relatively cheap brand that a helpful farmer allows us to buy wholesale, or, for competitive purposes, an excellent but considerably more expensive higher energy type produced under veterinary guidance.

As the ponies have their cubes mixed with boiled barley, the disadvantages of a low moisture content is overcome.

*OTHER ADDITIVES*

In the winter of 1977-78 the club was lucky to be presented with ten sacks of carrots, perfectly sound but jettisoned because by size and shape they did not conform to market requirements. They made a succulent addition to the ponies' diet, and were much appreciated. We worked up to a couple of pounds per head per day, and fed them washed and at first sliced lengthwise in the approved style. But slicing twelve pounds of carrots added greatly to the morning time factor, and eventually I accepted the advice that carrots can be safely fed whole—so long as they are not actually mixed in with the feed but put on the ground in a heap.

When the carrots came to an end we invested in a sack of "chat" potatoes. Washed but cooked in their skins, chopped almost to a mash, and mixed in with the feed, the quantity was slowly increased to substitute for a pound of cubes. They were not fed to Fiddler, but were particularly helpful in assuaging Jason's large appetite without increasing his natural exuberance.

On another occasion we had the gift of a few boxes of unwanted apples, and two or three of these cut up and added to the rations made a tasty addition to the diet. People quite often give us old, but fresh, cabbages or up-ended stalks of sprouts, and when grass is scarce this form of green meat is eaten eagerly.

Occasionally sugar-beet pulp is bought to make a change. As it swells when wet it is essential to soak the pulp overnight, and we introduce small quantities with caution. The ponies like it, but this is something else that Fiddler cannot tolerate.

### *MILK PELLETS*

These are very expensive indeed, but a little goes a long way. Only Paint and Briggy, both elderly gentlemen who tend to get a little "poor" in winter, have been given them; fed with caution and strictly according to the instructions, they acted as a good pick-me-up.

### *MINERALS AND SALT*

Although not all the ponies avail themselves of the facility, each field or shelter contains a mineral lick and, when we can come by it, a lump of the rock-salt that is always popular but not always available nowadays. In addition, a dessertspoonful of the old-fashioned "lump" cooking-salt—now often obtainable only from health food shops—is crumbled and stirred into the daily feeds.

### *DOLING OUT THE RATIONS*

At one time, when the club ponies numbered four and were fed only cubes in the way of concentrates, these were kept in the tack-room and members fed them to the ponies as and when directed. It seemed a good practice that they should be instrumental in this form of feeding, and for many months the plan worked well. Then I was away for a week and on my return was informed that Spotty had been very unlike his normal self out for a ride that day, so unwilling in fact that his rider had sensibly brought him straight home.

When I arrived at Spot's field the pony was reluctant to move at all, obviously distressed and sweating with pain. For a moment the awful idea that he had tetanus crossed my mind, but was dismissed as he had never missed out on his injections; inquiries from the worried members provided the clue to his malaise. It seemed that for the past week a clerical misunderstanding had resulted in Spot being fed his daily ration of cubes by three different people. Even then the total poundage did not add up to anything very great, but it was sufficient to produce what I suspected to be an acute attack of azoturia, a diagnosis confirmed by the vet.

Fortunately the pony quickly responded to an injection and, aided by the addition of bicarbonate of soda to his drinking water, within a week was back to normal—and there was no recurrence. But the incident decided me to keep all concentrated foods under my own jurisdiction. It was an isolated case and unlikely to happen again, but human nature being what it is there is always the chance that someone, some time, will slip their favourite a little extra. No harm may result, but with six ponies all being fed different quantities and in some cases different food, it seems safer not to tempt Providence. At weekends and during the holidays the members undertake this feeding, but each ration is doled out for them with the pony's name on a slip of paper.

### *ROUTINE*

All horses, physically and mentally, are geared to routine, particularly where feeding is concerned, and this is a rule of horsemastership with which we try to concur.

For some months during one winter Jason, Briggy, Amber and Fiddler were occupying the same field, and each morning at precisely eight o'clock could be seen lining the fence on the look-out for my van. Fiddler had to be fed separately anyway; also Briggy, since either Jason or Amber would gobble up their breakfast in order to drive him off his share.

All this called for some speedy moving on my part, and a quickly learned routine on that of the ponies. It meant dumping Jason's and Amber's buckets under the fence, and then legging it to the gate where the other two would be in a state of frustrated, and kicking, impatience. As the gate was opened they would both dive out, Fiddler turning sharp left to rush through a wicket where his breakfast awaited him, Briggy wheeling right to gallop fifty yards down the lane to the jumping field where his bucket was deposited.

*CHANGES IN DIET*

Possibly the club ponies have a change of diet more often than most because the type of concentrates they are given depends largely on the state of the club exchequer. And for this reason we take extra care in observing another golden rule of good feeding—to introduce different foods in very small quantities.

## *Chapter Nine*

# DAY TO DAY

SO FAR I have tried to put over something of what the Twala Club is all about and how it is run. Now is the time to try and show how the club operates from day to day, what the members get out of it and what, together with the ponies, they get up to.

### *VARYING INTERESTS*

Most evenings in summer, and most days in the holidays and weekends all year round, there is some form of pony activity going on around the schooling field or in the vicinity of the tack room across the lane. There are ponies being led or ridden bareback to and from their various fields, ponies hitched to the rail provided for the purpose alongside the field, ponies peering from the open shed where they are being groomed and saddled up, or stamping and whinnying at sight of an after-ride feed. It may be very early in the morning preparing for a show, or a Sunday when a lesson is imminent; some may be there to be trimmed, and one or two may have just returned from a country hack, the activity most in evidence with the club. Whatever is going on is usually, but not always, some form of communal effort.

If a club is to be one in the true sense of the word, members have to be prepared to get along with each other, and basically at least pull as a team in more or less the same direction. Obviously there are particular friendships and occasional tiffs and complaints, but an effort is made to keep rows about non-club matters outside its boundaries. On the other hand it would be unrealistic, and dull, to expect a dozen or more young people to share exactly the same riding interests, or hold exactly the same outlook where ponies are concerned. Different ambitions and viewpoints are appreciated, and furthered where possible.

*HACKING*

School terms or holidays, summer or winter, wet or fine, obviously the bulk of Twala Club time is devoted to going out for a ride, and is the facet most enjoyed by the majority. Usually they ride in pairs or groups, but there are the loners who prefer to ride by themselves—and are encouraged to do so once they reach a certain standard both in horsemanship and reliability.

Getting out on horseback by oneself teaches a lot of things besides self-reliance and is the best method of getting on terms with any pony, but there are occasional problems with diffident riders. It does tend to find the cracks in the armour of those who, when out with others, have been unwittingly relying on the herd instinct of horses to go along together.

Even the best-mannered pony is not above "trying it on" if it senses a rider's uncertainty; one young rider, a member of the club for some while but going out solo for the first time, discovered this for herself. She was partnering the admirable Amber, and no doubt he was well aware his rider was slightly overwhelmed at the thought of being out on her own. Anyway, they had scarcely covered a quarter of a mile before the pony stopped and, without making any real effort to make him continue on their way, his rider decided that Amber must be tired from previous, very normal exertions, turned him round, and came home.

When the story of this shortest of short rides came to light, it was pointed out that a pony is no fool, and that on that member's next outing by herself Amber would undoubtedly feel "tired" after half the previous distance—and if allowed to get away with it again might eventually consider himself too weary to start out at all!

## *ALARUMS AND EXCURSIONS*

Fortunately ninety-nine per cent of all rides produce nothing more out-of-the-way than varying degrees of enjoyment depending on route and weather, and to date our luck has held. Inevitably riders quite often fall off, and ponies and riders alike do stupid things, but, praise be, so far without serious consequences.

It was a bad moment one day when a neighbour rang to say that Fiddler had just been seen returning down the lane, at full gallop and without a rider. The caller had helpfully caught the pony and put him in the field, but there was no sign of the rider. This was worrying to say the least, and I went at once to investigate. At any rate Fiddler, who had been turned loose complete with tack, had refrained from rolling on his saddle or treading on his reins and was peacefully pulling at a hay net. But what of his rider? To my great relief, before very long she came in sight, trudging along, intact and apparently unperturbed at being jumped off by one of Fiddler's more spectacular leaps over a fallen tree-trunk. And again the luck was with us, in that the pony had emerged off a track at speed on to a comparatively busy country lane without either encountering a car or coming down.

On another occasion three quite novice members had to cope with what appeared to be a nasty situation, and acquitted themselves well. They were out with one of the associate members who was riding her Mrs. Plod, a sturdy little cob of much character, and weight. The party were cantering on the rough verge on either side of a metalled track when Plod caught a front foot in something that wrenched off the shoe, and sent the pony head over heels on top of her owner. It was a horrible fall, and the rider was knocked unconscious. It looked as though she must be badly injured, but no one panicked. The eldest girl took charge of the patient, and wisely did nothing but cushion her head on one anorak and cover her up with another. One member rode off to find a phone to summon parents and a doctor, another stationed herself at the top of the track to show them the way, and the youngest took charge of the surplus ponies.

They could not have acquitted themselves better and, thankfully, the incident had a better ending than seemed possible at the time. Although quite severely concussed and bruised from head to foot, the patient was on her feet again within a week—and riding out with Mrs. Plod within three.

## *LOCAL HAZARDS*

Every riding locality tends to produce its own particular perils, and our worst ones are fishermen's umbrellas, to which all our ponies take exception, and swans. Much of our best riding country encompasses some part or another of the tow-path alongside a canal, which not only attracts frequent anglers, but large congregations of swans who have made their home there.

The peculiar sound of swans in flight tends to produce some consternation amongst all new entries to the Twala Club stud, and care is taken to try and introduce the ponies to it from a distance. The racket of flapping and splashing generated by a mob of swans taking off from the water, followed by their sudden appearance within range of the equine eye, is something to which some of the ponies never become fully accustomed. Our riders have learned the hard way to sit tight and be prepared when the birds are about, but occasionally trouble manifests itself without warning.

In the very early days there was a boy member to whom the art of riding was to remain an insoluble mystery, and who was so nervous that eventually it seemed kinder to encourage him to find a pastime that involved remaining on his own two feet. Jabiska was the only animal up to his weight, and I was accompanying him one day, riding the redoubtable Spotty. It was to be a short and decorous ride, confined to walking and such trotting as seemed desirable, but the March wind was blowing in riotous gusts and even our placid Jabiska seemed to be a little on her toes. All went well, however, until we turned away from the tow-path to skirt an arable field, a route that would lead to a track and thence to the lane home.

And that was the moment when a horse's ability to see behind it, a gift not shared by its rider, was our undoing. Unheard amongst the bellowing of the wind six swans took off from the water directly behind us and flapped lustily into the ponies' range of vision. At the time I was holding forth on farming lore, and how it is essential on cultivated land to hug the fence and keep off any seeds or crops. Jabiska was in front and it is doubtful whether a word of this sage monologue could be heard, but the mare certainly heard and saw those swans. She stuck head and tail in the air and took off across the field at a speed that would have left me gasping, if I had not been fully occupied with troubles of my own. Her wake looked as though a herd of elephant had stampeded that way.

The mare's rider appeared to be too frozen with horror to fall off. And that was as well because the impossible-to-project shouts of advice and encouragement I was then endeavouring to waft his way were soon swallowed up by pleas to Spotty, doing his utmost to match his friend's racing pace, at least to remain on course beside the fence, and to refrain from bucking me off.

Jabiska ran out of steam eventually and stopped, her rider still miraculously in the saddle. And the farmer concerned was subsequently either unable to believe his eyes when he saw her most apparent flight-path, or failed to find out who was responsible. But although that particular Twala Club member left us soon after for pastures new, we still meet up occasionally. And then he advances, eyes shining with recollection, to say: "We didn't half gallop that day, didn't we!"

There is another favourite ride that starts off by the canal and then meanders up across the hills along a bridle-path. And since that right-of-way cuts through the outlying acres of a wild-life sanctuary, the ponies have to cope with hazards not normally encountered in the English countryside. If one or another of them starts to snort suspiciously while still on the tow-path, that means that the water-buffalo are inhabiting

20. *One of the joys of belonging to a club—hacking out together.*

their most favoured wallow close by. They are peaceful, harmless beasts (from the other side of the fence at any rate), but it must be owned they do not smell like cows and none of the ponies ever seem to get entirely used to this aroma. On the way up over the hills, if the ponies suddenly set off at speed that means that the Przevalski stallion and his harem are galloping up behind, although safely on their side of the fence. One of our riders met the stallion face-to-face on the bridle-path on one momentous occasion, but managed to beat a strategic retreat.

Fiddler normally pays little attention to any of these strange creatures, but one of our boys had a lengthy argument with him on the day he was riding alone and a fine male wapiti hove in sight. The pony made it very plain that no self-respecting horse should be asked to pass something carrying head embellishments like that.

Further on, when the wind is blowing in the wrong direction, the entire Twala Club pony group is liable to come to a halt in the middle of the road, with ears tight pricked, eyes bolting out of their heads and nostrils flared to catch a horrifying scent. What they can smell is the pack of wolves that inhabits a nearby section of pine wood, and since the ponies' instinctive reactions can be unsafe in traffic, an illicit short cut through the sanctuary car park is usually taken.

### *ROUTES*

There are lovely rides around this countryside but they are limited in number. A favoured one with the better riders, especially the boys, comprises an adventurous trek along the hillsides and over the hunt jumps and intersecting streams. Another never-failing joy for riders and ponies alike is to make their way down to the sea. When the tide is right there are vast areas of sand to canter on, breakwaters and little pools to jump, and the exhilaration of splashing through spray on the edge of the water. Horse-riders have unlimited access to the sands from the end of September round to the beginning of May, but for the remainder of the year horses are restricted to any time between eight o'clock in the evening and eight a.m. the following morning.

*BREAKFAST ON THE SANDS*

This summer embargo has led to one of the most popular Twala Club doings of the year—the picnic breakfast down by the sea. Owing to the British climate such an affair is not always possible since a fine hot day is required to coincide with a low tide. But when all is well everyone puts on bathing attire under their jeans, a contingent sets off with the ponies around 5 a.m., and the remainder follow on by car with any parents who like to be included. The same site, sheltered by a groyne, is usually chosen because it provides shelter from sea-breezes. It also provides the first bit of equestrian fun, when some of the more reluctant ponies have to be persuaded around the sea end of the edifice and through a shallow turbulence of water draining off the marshes. Once this is achieved, while another posse of riders goes for a canter along the sands, everyone else busies themselves collecting driftwood to make a fire for cooking quantities of sausages and bacon, cutting mounds of bread, butter and marmalade and boiling the kettle for tea.

There is nowhere to tie the ponies, so they are well in on the picnic and apparently as ravenous as their riders! With breakfast over and the site cleared up, and in theory at least a hot sun and warm sea to hand, the human element strips down to their bathing necessities, the ponies to their head-collars, and everyone ventures into the water, some people with a four-legged companion.

Each pony reacts differently to the idea. Paint will only paddle fetlock-deep, Jason and Amber will go happily in up to their bellies. To date sea-bathing is an unknown quantity as far as Taffy and Pinocchio are concerned, and Fiddler is usually the star-turn—quite willing to swim out with the boys.

The time creeps on towards 8 a.m. and it is the moment to leave; ponies dry out on the return journey, and this is the end of an outing that never palls.

### *THE CREATORS*

The older boys enjoy excursions like that as much as everyone else, but although they like unadorned hacking to a degree, they tend to get bored without some sort of objective—be it jumping across country or in the interests of getting a pony fit for a competition. And unlike the girls, the boys relish constructing amenities for the club.

They are responsible for the two sets of uprights that together with a miscellany of barrels support our home jumps. One of them painted all the poles, white washed and numbered the small barrels used as dressage-markers, and contrived two different-sized and realistic "walls", from a couple of doors painted with red bricks. One boy built up quite a formidable log-pile—a construction not improved when he and Jason promptly hit it and fell flat at a first attempt to jump it.

In our earliest days, all the ponies entered in one microscopic jumping-class got round in stages to the last obstacle, a miniature pit at which they stopped and stared with horror. So the boys returned home and dug a practice-pit for the Twala Club—with which the ponies would still not have anything to do, until for some days they found the only way to reach their breakfast was to jump in and get it. Not so long ago the near promise of a rosette was lost through unfamiliarity with a water-jump. And once again the boys came to the rescue, digging out a comparable hazard of the correct dimensions and lining it with plastic sheeting which remains water-tight long enough to jump.

### *SCHOOLING FACILITIES*

It is lucky that the three-quarters of an acre used for schooling and jumping is flat, and the soil light and quick-drying so that, barring ice or snow, or after endless days of torrential rain, it is always usable. It has lately been adorned with a stout hitching-rail down one side, and an area for parking cars and boxing ponies when we are loaned a trailer—much appreciated amenities constructed by the club fathers.

21. *Jumping in and out of a pit is good practice for competing across country.*

Despite its small size the field has a number of hunter-trial type fences round the perimeter, including a "live" hedge that was growing well and the pride of its originator until Jason sat down in the middle of it. A dressage arena has been marked out, and cunningly contrived so that there is still room for schooling on a large rectangular track, and for our variety of makeshift show-jumps.

In addition to the official instruction, the field is used by members for schooling on their own, jumping practice, and for having a bit of fun with gymkhana games when there is no time to ride out. It is also a suitable venue for those capable of lunging—an art which has been confined strictly to the older and more experienced since the day I was lunging Fiddler over fences and landed directly behind him instead of to the side, full in the line of fire when he exuberantly kicked back.

From the members' point of view the only drawback to this field is the fact that it is in view from our house, perched on an adjacent hill. And if anything untoward is going on I am liable to see it and descend on the culprits like an unwelcome avenging angel!

## *INSTRUCTION*

One of the club's greatest assets is the acquisition of a young, qualified instructor who, without intending to, has become so involved with the set-up that her help and interest extend way beyond any official hours. Officially she teaches the club at weekends, the lesson given indoors with theory replacing practical work if the weather is really impossible. Otherwise, winter and summer alike she gives the members, divided into two rides and with club associates usually joining in, a couple of hours of lively, informed instruction in return for a nominal fee and the occasional use of a pony.

During the holidays extra lessons are squeezed in where possible, and special help given to those wishing to make an attempt at Pony Club eventing or other unfamiliar enterprises.

22. *Correct instruction is a "must" for this type of club.*

Members are taught the intricacies of correct trimming, and "pulling" of manes and tails, and ponies "sorted out" as required. In the early hours of a competing day our instructor is more than likely to turn up, happy to lend a hand with anything from shampooing a pony's tail to supervising the leg-bandaging before travelling. She is there at the show, to take charge of the lesser lights if required, walk a course and advise on the best approach, or battle with Pinocchio in a suitable class if he happens to be having an off day.

Occasionally the weekly lesson takes the form of cross-country instruction, on an estate and over a course known to and appreciated by my own family many years ago. This facility is four or five miles away and the exercise commonly takes up much of the day, comprising a leisurely hack over there with one set of riders and back again with another, with a rest for the ponies and a picnic for the riders after the jumping is finished.

These fences were unused for many years, but with some help

from the club have now been renovated. And it is a joy to see our present bunch of ponies tackling, or not as the case may be, all the same hazards that Twala and our other family ponies learned to cope with a long time ago—the miniature coffin in the drainage-patch, the drop into the heifers' field, the hedge that appears formidable until you have jumped it. The drop down a bank into the little river still presents a problem for most, and it took a couple of daily sessions and a lot of effort and coaxing to persuade Jason and Pinocchio that the feat was possible. Paint once caused a scare by slipping into the dry ditch on the far side of the stile, lying there winded and immovable until a bucket of food was produced.

Access to facilities like this, and to the range of other people's show-jumps that are sometimes available, provide invaluable training for competitions, and give a fillip to more routine instruction for everyone, competitive-minded or not.

## *VALUE OF INSTRUCTION*

To my mind instruction, imparted by someone who is both qualified in the subject and accustomed to young people, is vital to the success of the club and any comparable venture, if the project is to aim higher than merely providing a cheap source of riding. It is essential for stimulating over-all interest, furthering ambition, however slight, and satisfying the wish to learn more of a subject that is as fascinating as it is inexhaustible. Inevitably the aims, as the abilities, vary with the individuals, but it is both exciting and rewarding to look back and realize just how far our present club members have come from the original non-existent standards and to appreciate just how much benefit the ponies derive from their riders' increasing knowledge and efficiency.

## *PONY CLUB*

For the past two years the Twala Club instruction has been furthered and the field of competition much extended, by our joining the official Pony Club. This was previously impracticable because of transport problems and the fact that until recently all the working rallies were held outside hacking distance. Directly two or three were organized in our area some of our members joined at once, the number restricted to match the number of ponies. Now, however, all but two belong to the Pony Club and take it in turns to attend available rallies.

As our own instructor also instructs for the Pony Club, the tuition is along the same lines, and working for the efficiency tests and competing at the organization's level present more and most welcome objectives and challenges. It is rewarding, and says a lot for our instructor that to date all Twala Clubbers

23. *The more experienced help out the novices.*

have passed their D and C tests with flying colours at the first attempt. And two members and one associate are having a go at their B tests a year after gaining C. Whether they pass what is nowadays quite a stiff examination in horsemanship is another matter, but they would not have been nominated for the attempt unless Pony Club officials considered them to be somewhere near the required standard.

### *CAMP*

Membership of the Pony Club has opened up many vistas for Twala Clubbers, including the adventure of going to camp. Recently for the first time two members, taking Pinocchio and Taffy, were able to sample the fun of communal life combined with the concentrated daily instruction that makes up the Pony Club programme, and affords the chance to benefit from practical stable-management. The ponies appeared to enjoy themselves as much as their riders, and the week was of mutual benefit.

### *BRIDLEWAYS ASSOCIATION*

It is club policy to be on the look out for new ventures, and since I am a static member of this Association our members are able to join in the occasional ride on payment of a nominal fee.

Ponies being what they are and, like children, most likely to let you down on the special occasion, it was rash to have given the assurance that ours are all well-behaved. Within minutes of meeting up with the Bridleways horsemen, Jason, only known to lift a hind-leg under the intoxication of first seeing hounds, decided that this was a new form of hunting and had hastily to be relegated to the position of tail-end Charlie. Within seconds of "moving off" the young pony belonging to our associate had bucked off his rider and disappeared in the opposite direction, sportingly pursued by a contingent of our hosts. He was eventually caught and re-mounted, and after that things settled down. It proved an enjoyable excursion—and the Twala Club has not been banned from future rides.

24. *Twala club ponies are expected to do anything. Medieval costumes of ponies and riders for a local pageant, all made by the instructor and members.*

## *OTHER DIVERSIONS*

Some years ago our local section of Southern TV made a short feature film of the club, an experience that the present members would love to have repeated. The number of "takes" necessary for each episode, the number of hours expended to produce a few minutes of usable film, were an eye-opener to the riders—and the producer had the utmost co-operation from them and the ponies. And the thrill and pride of seeing themselves "on the box" is something that those who took part will never forget.

Occasionally the club finds itself involved in special photography for book illustrations, as with this one, and that again is a source of fun and interest.

Before increasing traffic made riding in the dark too

hazardous, the ponies were always included at Christmas in the house-to-house carol-singing that used to benefit some charity and provide a small percentage for the club.

Recently the Twala Club was asked to produce a medieval group to ride in a local pageant. And with the combined efforts of the club and instructor, an authentically accoutred group of riders and horses duly presented themselves on the day. A knight bestrode his destrier, Jason, accompanied by his squire carrying lance and shield and riding Fiddler, one of the least likely to be perturbed by these appendages. The knight's lady, elegantly mounted side-saddle on a mildly surprised Pinocchio, was attended by her page on Amber, and a prosperous burgher and his wife, carried respectively by Taffy and Paint, evidently happy with a side-saddle, completed the entourage.

## *HUNTING*

The decision to participate in the sport of fox-hunting was deferred for several reasons until quite recently.

To begin with, it is only in the past two years or so that any of our riders became capable of coping in the hunting-field, and once they were there was still the question of the ponies.

Before coming to us Amber had been hunted for many seasons and was renowned as a super little hunter, but he is the kind more likely to be heading the field than content to stay behind in the rut. He would give the maximum fun to an experienced young rider, but was he quite the pony for someone totally uninitiated in hunting lore? As far as was known Jason had never seen hounds in his life and, judging by his normal exuberance when jumping or at speed in company, was likely to be a very strong ride. Paint would have been very suitable and would know what he was about, but it was felt he would take too much out of himself. Briggy was known to be controllable—so long as he was not held up at a fence, where his impatient cat-leaping could be distinctly unseating. Taffy was not yet with us; he is still an unknown quantity in the hunting-field, but predictably would be a bit of a handful for a novice.

Pinocchio had never hunted in his life. It was difficult to imagine him livening up to the point of being unmanageable or hard to hold, but one can never tell. Sometimes the heady mixture of horse and hound can prove even more intoxicating to the very quiet animal than to something normally on its toes.

Fiddler seemed the only sure bet. He had been hunted quietly as a four-year-old before we had him, and had been proved mannered, and amenable to going first or last as required.

So much for the ponies, but apart from these considerations there was the question of the members' attitudes towards field sports. One of the boys is always keen to try a new experience, another was in two minds only because he is by nature diffident about the unknown. With the exception of the one who loves to tackle anything so long as it is connected with a pony, all the girls declared themselves unequivocally anti-"blood-sport".

It would be unwarranted for a club like this to exert undue pressure on what could well be a family issue, and everyone is entitled to their own opinion—so long, to my way of thinking, as their views are founded on personal or reliably informed experience of some sort and not merely on biased hearsay. It appeared that the Twala Clubbers' objections were based almost entirely on the reports that appear at intervals in the most prejudiced "anti" sections of the press, supplemented by their own over-vivid imaginations.

It seemed a pity if these young people were to bypass the opportunity for making up their own minds on the subject. There was also the fact that the hunting-field is the best possible school, both for horse and rider, for those interested in hunter trials and eventing, and this is something that was pointed out. Otherwise the matter was left in abeyance.

And then, early one October morning not so long ago, three Twala Club ponies were saddled up and trotted off to a cubbing meet some four miles away.

There was one of the boys riding Fiddler, and our enthusiastic girl member with Amber, accompanied by our instructor, who had undertaken to look after them and at the same time try out Jason's reactions to fox-hunting—with the precautionary addition of a running martingale on one end of the cob and a red ribbon on the other.

It had been decided to arrive in good time, to give the ponies a chance to take a look at hounds and settle down, and the two young riders to imbibe something of the atmosphere and to recall something of the etiquette and rules with which they had been primed. Inevitably the trek took longer than envisaged and their first introduction to the sport came as they rounded a corner—to meet huntsman, hounds and field head on.

Considering all things the ponies behaved well, even Jason who was too amazed at that point to think up anything. In fact he had little option as all three were hastily tucked tail first into the hedge while the pack went by, and almost as soon as they managed to infiltrate into the field the huntsman switched off the lane to draw a patch of kale.

It was near to the opening meet, and the strong cub that broke covert was not held up, but allowed to provide what turned out to be a good little run and an exciting initiation into the sport. True to form, Amber showed a turn of speed that took him past most of the field, but as he never faltered at the two or three fences encountered and his manners are impeccable, there was no cause for complaint and his rider was given an exhilarating taste of the excitements of the chase. Fiddler, still slightly below par, did all that was required to show his rider enjoyable sport. As expected Jason took some holding, and at one stage his rider was seen negotiating a gateway at a pace that was surely unintended; but he settled much quicker than anticipated and obviously found the morning to his liking.

On their return the two foxhunters were closely questioned about every aspect of the day, including a kill that happened so quickly it was over before they realized what had occurred. And as a result of their report, more members expressed a wish to hunt and find out for themselves what happens.

By the end of that season all those capable of hunting had

experienced the sport at least once. There had been good days and blank days. One of our associates, out on her own, was reported by the field-master to have been totally out of control, but blissfully happy and in nobody's way. The boys hunted Jason successfully, but one was not popular when leading the Twala Club party he omitted to give the aid to take off over a hurdle: the cob failed to notice the obstacle and reduced it to matchwood—and it was to prove the only jumpable fence of the day.

Most of the aspirants who were too big for Amber wished to hunt Fiddler, a great confidence-giver whatever the size of fence—while Pinocchio, directly he was added to the list of hunters, proved invaluable. Neither horn nor hounds nor the thrills of galloping in company stirs him one jot or tittle. He proceeds at his normal speeds regardless, jumps if he wishes to, and can be trusted to carry a complete novice in utter safety.

No one would suggest that as yet these young people know much about the nuances of a sport so new to them, but they know sufficient to acknowledge that hunting bears small resemblance to their preconceived ideas, and all of them concluded that first season looking forward eagerly to the next and to learning more about hound-work and the ways of the fox.

Hunting can occur only on those days when the meets are within hacking distance, but the sport has added a new dimension to the activities of the Twala Club.

## *Chapter Ten*

# COMPETING

IT MIGHT BE misconstrued and seem disappointing that our competing seasons now bring fewer rosettes to adorn the tack room wall than in the first couple of years of club participation, but in truth that is a sign of the way the riders have progressed.

The shows we now attend are not the large affairs run under B.S.J.A. rules and approaching "county" status, but they are on a different level to those at which the Twala Club first flexed its competitive muscles. And nowadays the competition is so hot, the standard getting higher every year, that even unaffiliated and Pony Club competing at moderate grades calls for quite high-class performers, both two legged and four. All of which adds up to the fact that a rosette, no higher than third or fourth, takes considerably more winning than a first or a second in days gone by, and is to be assessed more highly.

### *OLD STYLE*

There was a time, long past, when all the Twala Club girls liked to enter for Best Turned Out classes, though not necessarily because either they or their ponies qualified for the competition. (A judge was once heard imploring one of our entrants, "Just try *one* little plait next time . . . then perhaps we could give you something"!) Their reason for entering was because of the decorous pace required—no request to go faster than a walk, and therefore no ponies likely to take off. But, if nothing else, the class did give them a little flavour of the show ring.

### *SHOW JUMPING*

Most shows put on so many different grades of the sport that there is usually some class to suit all our ponies and riders, except the complete novices—and they can always make a start with the popular Clear Round jumping.

The club normally gets to one or two indoor shows during the winter. Indoors or outside, Fiddler and Amber can usually be relied on to produce clear rounds in their respective classes, even if they are then defeated "against the clock". Pinocchio can partner his rider to a competent first round, and Taffy, like Jason, has a lot of potential. When Paint is finally retired there is hope we may be able to acquire another 14.2 novice all-rounder, and that will relieve the pressure on the other better ponies, and provide more chances for the more ambitious riders.

There was the cherished occasion when Jabiska, whose past history was never known, entered a jumping competition. She came in to jump while a thunderstorm rumbled overhead, streaks of lightning sent some of the competitors' ponies plunging in fright, and the rain bucketed down to turn the arena into a skid-pan. Despite the conditions, all the young competitors had been determined to have their money's worth, and though ponies skidded on the corners and almost slipped up there were no serious incidents. They had, however, also been slithering into the little fences, and by the time Jabiska, last to go, trotted soberly into the ring there had not yet been one clear round.

As far as we were concerned this was her debut in show-jumping, just as it most palpably was that of her pale-faced rider. Yet it seemed to us, watching with bated breath from the side-lines, that Jabiska had an ear cocked for the signal to start, and if, as some swore, she was heeding the onlookers' shouted advice as to what fence came next, she would still have done the whole job just as easily without a rider. She knew exactly what she was about, and kept to a steady, clumping trot that combined with her normal up-and-down action and big feet to hold her balanced on corners and approaches alike. No fence was more than two feet high, but under those conditions Jabiska dealt with them all with extreme caution, slowing almost to a stop before heaving herself over. She steadied again on landing, and no one would have been very surprised is she had then twisted her head round to inquire if her rider was still up top!

By the time they arrived at the last fence, still unpenalized, the tension was almost unbearable, but Aunt Jabiska made it—to clop out of the ring in a blaze of deserved glory. And though her rider was to win quite an assortment of prizes in the years to come, none of them meant more than that bedraggled red rosette tied to Jabiska's brow-band in the middle of a thunderstorm.

Soon little shows like that one, where no one was expected to go home without at least one "consolation" rosette, were being replaced by slightly bigger, slightly better, ones. The boys had quickly imbibed a liking for gymkhana games, and some of the required speed and toughness. Sometimes they were successful, and it was then that it was first discovered that Spotty was almost unbeatable at barrel-jumping—the only pony of my acquaintance who will jump a single small barrel of his own volition.

Then as now, riders fell off, failed to go through start or finish, set off before the whistle, or took the wrong course, and ponies jumped one day and decided not to on the next. Those were the days when by some miracle Paint won the First for jumping—as far as he was concerned a non-repeatable feat—that ever after precluded him from most of the classes for which he is fitted. Jabiska reached the last obstacle in an "in and out of the ring" kind of cross-country, only to suffer a mutual failure of nerve with her rider and demolish the fence beyond repair.

## *OUTLOOK*

Like everyone else in the game, the Twala Clubbers have suffered, and learned to live with, all the frustrations and near misses, the bumps and tumbles that go along with competing with ponies. There was the occasional win and more frequent "place" to spur them on in the early years, highlights like the day Spot reached three-foot-six in the Chase-me-Charlie to come second—and bucked his boy rider off during each circuit to the jump. For most of them, win or lose, the fun and excitement has become irresistible. They may not be able to do any of it very often, the material rewards may not be numerous, but the sights are always set for new fields to conquer; to "have a go", regardless of results, is the objective.

## *HUNTER TRIALS*

In Fiddler's second year with us we took him to some novice hunter trials. It was a first try for the pony, and on the way there his boy rider was heard to inquire what a hunter trial was, exactly? On arrival the rider was walked round the course, entered in his appropriate age class, and came eighth out of thirty-six entries.

We lost our heads and entered the same partnership for the Open, still of no great standard but involving a number of big horses and riders up to eighteen years old. It was suggested that Fiddler might be given a slap as they set off to wake him up a bit, but although the resulting gallop did not look exactly speedy, the pair returned looking happy. No, they had not gone very fast, but Fiddler had taken the fences in his stride and did not seem to alter his pace the whole way round. Everyone was pleased about their going clear, and neither pony nor rider seemed to have been aware that some of the fences had been put up to 3′ 6″. We all went home, and not long afterwards there was a phone message to say that Fiddler had won by quite an impressive margin.

To date, that stout effort has not been repeated and may never be again, but it was a far cry from the club's first ever hunter trial. This was another memorable occasion, when Paint set the ball rolling by depositing his rider three times in the same section of muddy stream before being disqualified. It was Spot, however, who, not for the first time, crowned the day. His rider was a newly joined young member who, unlike our other newcomers, had been riding for a year or two. What no one realized was that competing was a totally new venture, both to herself and to her parents who had come to cheer her on. As she and Spot made their way down to the start the pony looked to be bouncing around in an unfamiliar fashion, but I failed to notice that his rider, in a fluster of nerves, was unwittingly holding him in a vice while her heels were jammed into his sides.

They set off at a pace not normally associated with Twala Club doings and cleared the first two fences as though point-to-pointing. At that moment my attention was distracted. When I looked again it was to see Spot off-course and returning to base, ears flat, tail on high, his rider hanging on for dear life but with legs drawn back and heels still rammed into the pony's sides.

Spot was making for the collecting-ring behind me, a narrow entrance where ponies were to-ing and fro-ing, and stupidly I

25. *The pairs class in a hunter trial is an excellent school for pony and rider.*

made a move to stop him. What happened next is not entirely clear but he must have taken the wrong evasive action, and we collided.

It was a painful and rather ridiculous experience, but my own embarrassment was nothing compared to that of our new recruit and her parents, proudly making their first appearance in public with the Twala Club . . . only to floor the principal!

*EVENTING*

Hunter trials soon became a popular form of competing with some of our better riders, and when membership of the Pony Club made eventing an exciting possibility it was helpful to have already gleaned a little about riding across country.

Dressage, as such, was an unknown quantity, little more than a foreign-sounding word to be skimmed over in the horse books, and our first-line participants are very lucky indeed to have their basic schooling occasionally supplemented by help from an expert.

Obviously knowledge and performance is still completely in its infancy, but at least they now have an idea of what they are trying to achieve, and why, and how to set about it, both from their own point of view and from that of their ponies.

In Jason's first season, the betting on his remaining in the dressage arena at his first and only appearance, was two to one against—and most of the test was performed at the gallop, which gave the judges a hectic time trying to mark the movements! Now he is supple, established in a good walk and a quite impressive rhythmic trot, even if his canter can still be reminiscent of the race-track. He is now capable of a respectable attempt at novice level, and it is bad luck that the age of the boy who events him compels them to compete in the senior classes—unless there is the rare chance to ride *hors concours* at the lower level. This age difficulty is a legacy of joining the Pony Club "late in life".

Eventing is not for everyone, and the sport does present special problems for a club run on Twala Club lines. Apart

26. *It was a long haul from the start of the club to eventing—but it can be done!*

from the age question, ponies and riders must work and compete together as partners for at least part of a season, unlike the show-jumping and gymkhana competitions where it is feasible to swap around in the interests of giving everyone a turn. But for those who have both the ability and the chance, this is the most challenging and satifying, if demanding, form of competition—win or lose. And a rider and pony who can complete all three phases of a one-day event, whatever the level, are on the road to proving their worth.

### *PONY CLUB TETRATHLON*

When the club first began competing, mention of a contest that involved pistol-shooting, swimming, riding across country and running, would not have evoked the smallest interest, yet one reason for eventually joining the Pony Club was a particular Twala Clubber's delight at discovering that such a challenge existed.

Aims of this kind are always to be encouraged, but once again the age problem crept in. The enthusiast concerned was a boy coming up for sixteen, with exams looming, after which he would be leaving school to take a job. If he were to have a go it had to be that season, and as it was he would have to compete as a senior, though it would be a novice tetrathlon. Nothing daunted, he found someone to teach him to shoot and, a conscientious character, took all the training very seriously. Each evening found him slogging round the countryside, swimming increasing distances, or riding Fiddler, if no one else wanted to, as part of their mutual get-fit programme.

It was a two-day competition and on the first day, understandably nervous, he found that his shooting was not quite up to his usual form. Not being a speed-merchant at swimming, the encouraging second place he gained—after a South African boy who must have been born in the water—was due to sheer, dogged determination.

In the cross-country riding section we had been told that the fences would be no higher than 3′ 6″, a height well within Fiddler's normal scope. But the spreads were big and sadly the pony was not "normal". He had been, as we thought, prepared as carefully as possible for an animal that lives out, and he looked splendid. But his constitution could not cope with the extra food and, unsuspected, one of his slight attacks of azoturia had flared up, and our competitor was out at the third fence.

Last season another boy was contemplating entering with Jason, but postponed the idea as he had a year in hand and the cob needed more time. Our sole entrant this year is therefore a small eleven-year-old, chosen for the Pony Club junior tetrathlon team. The swimming and running may be a bit of a problem, but his shooting is adequate and Amber should take care of the cross-country riding section.

A tetrathlon is an excellent challenge for the boys. It may

be aiming high for an association such as the Twala Club, but win or lose the incentive is a first-class inducement to train for a variety of sports.

## *TRANSPORT*

Whatever the competition, the Club's chief drawback to participating remains the difficulty in getting there. To add to the problem, since Fiddler's frightening attack of claustrophobia on a long journey in the trailer that is loaned to us, we are hesitant about trying him again for any distance in a vehicle that is not our own. Since that day he has travelled without trouble with other ponies in a horsebox, and also quite happily on his own in the trailer without a partition. That is normal behaviour for horses with the same problem, but does not solve our difficulties when we want to use the trailer to go to a show en masse, and two journeys is the limit.

Fiddler still goes into a trailer without hesitation and, convinced that his "claustrophobia" was in part due to his state of mild debility at the time, I decided to carry out an experiment. This had to be done on the metalled roads on a private estate—it is against the law for anyone to travel inside with a horse on a highway—and with our usual loaned trailer as it has a large space in front of the ponies' heads where I could stand. (This last is essential, and the idea should not be contempleted by anyone who is not fully experienced.) There was someone in the back of the Landrover to keep an eye on things and tell the driver to stop if necessary.

Fiddler was bandaged with layers of gamgee stretching down below his fetlocks, and a tail-guard over a tail-bandage. The imperturbable Pinocchio was chosen as a travelling companion. I had Fiddler's breakfast in a bucket, and stood within his reach in front of the forward bars. He was eating as we set off, as smoothly as possible, but immediately tensed, laid back his ears and started to sit down. I seized his head-collar and pulled and shouted at him, and as he responded offered him food. He began to eat and relax, but every time we took a right-handed bend started to lose his legs and threatened to go down sideways. Each time I managed to prevent him going right down by pulling and bawling "No! Get UP!", and gradually he began to keep his feet and continue eating. Instead of straddling his legs he had been keeping the hind ones close together, but as we proceeded began to get the idea, and with growing confidence the traumatic moments grew less frequent.

By the end of half-an-hour the improvement was sufficient to bear out my theory, at least to some extent. And during the latter part of our experiment my worries were less with Fiddler than with Pinocchio, frustrated at the sight of a meal he could not share and making known his displeasure with his teeth.

That was an unpleasant and at intervals frightening experience and one I am not anxious to repeat, but it convinced me that with time and much patience such a problem can be solved. Come the autumn school term we are hoping to be able to borrow the trailer for a week or two. Then we can make a short journey each day, possibly with the pony facing

27. *A big feather in this boy rider's cap—Jason now goes across country.*

out of the back, and see if we can reach the stage once more when Fiddler is a happy traveller in company.

Our dream is eventually to acquire some kind of vehicle in reasonable repair, that could be converted into a small horse-box to carry three or four ponies. Whether the club will ever achieve this, or have the finances to keep it on the road if they do, is problematical, but it would put a different complexion on our competing ambitions.

### *BOXING*

It is little use having the means to travel if the ponies refuse to utilize it, but most problems connected with persuading them to go into a trailer can be overcome by familiarity and repetition of the manœuvre. As the Twala Club only has a trailer on the premises at intervals, any troubles can be that much more difficult to overcome, but so far none has proved insurmountable.

Spot, having "boxed" happily for years, suddenly started declining to go into a trailer if he could help it. On the day he was setting off to join his new family, this super little pony at sight of their trailer spent some twenty minutes plunging and standing on his hind legs. In the end we were forced to put on a saddle and attach the head-collar rope, through his front legs, to the girth so that he could not rear. It was then possible to lift him in, and a relief to hear later that his new owners had solved the problem in a very short while—by feeding Spot first on the ramp and then inside the trailer, and then consolidating the idea by frequently leading him in and out.

When a friend undertook to collect Jason from his previous home, the cob proceeded as far as halfway up the ramp and then, quite benignly, refused to budge. We had tried everything we could think of, including a bucket of oats, without result, when Jason's owner suddenly appeared inside the trailer and opened up her handbag. In a flash the big palomino was inside, exploring the bag for the peppermints that are his particular weakness.

He now boxes as easily as Amber or Fiddler. Taffy makes no difficulties about the matter either, but has to be tied up short to stop him nipping his travelling companion. If he has not been boxed recently Paint can be stubborn about the idea, but yields gracefully to the application of a couple of lunging reins tied either side of the trailer, crossed above his hocks, and gently pulled. Pinocchio can be very mulish if he feels like it, but the lunge reins, plus the application of the business end of a garden broom if necessary, have not failed as yet to make him comply.

Competing is not everything, and certainly only a part of what the Twala Club is all about. But on one hand our increasing successes could be looked on as a mark of the long way the club has come, at least competing-wise, in the six years since it was formed. On the other hand the rest of it merely confirms that ponies, like their riders, can be unpredictable—and life might well become too serious if they were not!

How long the Twala Club will continue, it is impossible to surmise. Chiefly that depends on two factors: finances and the enthusiasm of its members. And if each year finds the monetary side more difficult, we shall still probably manage to muddle through because to date the keenness and interest shown by all those concerned act as a constant spur.

It could be that the story of some of the Twala Club's tribulations seem to overshadow the joys, which might scare off someone contemplating a similar scheme, but I hope not. For myself it will be a very sad day when my life ceases to be enriched, and occasionally bedevilled, by all the delightful young people and ponies who have been a part of it for these happy years.

# INDEX